The Complete Guide to
CLAYPOT
COOKING

BRIDGET JONES

Photography by
JAMES DUNCAN

a Salamander book
Published by Salamander Books Limited
LONDON • NEW YORK

Published by Salamander Books Limited
129 – 137 York Way, London N7 9LG,
United Kingdom

© Salamander Books Ltd 1993

Distributed by Reco International Corp.
150 Haven Ave.,
Port Washington,
N.Y. 11050

This book was created by Tones

Art Director: Jo Tapper
Editor: Alison Leach
Home Economists: Joanna Farrow and Sara Lewis
Stylist: Madeleine Brehaut
Colour Separation by: Scantrans Pte. Ltd.
Printed in Belgium by Proost International Book Production

The publishers would like to thank the following for the loan
of clay pots for testing and photography:
Romertopf International
William Levene Ltd
Reco International Corp.

Notes
All spoon measures are equal.
1 teaspoon = 5ml spoon
1 tablespoon = 15ml spoon.

CONTENTS

INTRODUCTION

Using terracotta pots for cooking is one of the oldest traditions which dates back to Roman times, when the first great gourmets appreciated the fine results which could be obtained by soaking clay pots before cooking in them. The soaked pots absorb water which generates moisture during cooking to create a unique baking environment which calls for the minimum use of fat and results in the maximum flavor. The pot keeps food superbly moist, at the same time encouraging flavors to mingle and preventing rapid overcooking. Basting is largely unnecessary and the covered pot prevents roasts from drying out. While the pot ensures succulent results, the oven is kept free from the usual splashing and spitting associated with most roasting. The versatile clay pot may be used for making a wide variety of dishes, from soups and stews to desserts and breads. You will also find recipes which show how to use the clay pot in the microwave cooker. Read through the essential information which follows, then sample the pleasures of dining claypot style.

COOKING IN CLAY

Claypot cookery is, in essence, a means of creating full-flavored dishes with the minimum of effort. It does not involve complicated preparation or specialist techniques but there are a few basic rules which should be followed at all times. It is important to follow the manufacturer's instructions to prevent damage and to ensure success.

PREPARING THE CLAY POT FOR COOKING

Wash a new pot in hand-hot water adding a little mild dishwashing liquid, and rinse it thoroughly.

The clay pot must be soaked for 15 minutes before use.

Soaking The first step in preparing a claypot recipe is to soak the pot in cold water for 15 minutes, or until you are ready to put the food in the pot. If the pot has never been used before, it should be soaked for 30 minutes. Place the pot and lid in the sink or in a washing-up bowl. Invert the lid on top of the pot to save space and fill the sink or bowl with cold water to completely submerge the pot and lid.

The unglazed, porous pot absorbs water during soaking. As the pot heats in the oven, the water which it has absorbed evaporates to create a moist cooking atmosphere. Not only does this prevent foods from drying out but it also encourages suitable ingredients to create a flavorsome cooking liquor.

The moist atmosphere promotes tender results when roasting meat and preserves the natural flavor of foods such as seafood, poultry, meat and vegetables. When used for baking, the pot encourages items, such as cakes and breads, to rise well. The pot also helps to give yeasted bread a good crust which further crisps when the lid is removed for the final 10 minutes or so of cooking.

The material and moisture which is retained in the pot makes it unnecessary to add fat for basic cooking. For example, meat and poultry may be roasted without any additional fat and fish or smaller cuts

Base-lined clay pot for baking bread.

of meat and poultry may be baked without adding oil or butter if wished.

Bottom Lining When cooking baked items, such as bread or cakes, it makes sense to line the bottom of the clay pot with a piece of non-stick baking parchment. This ensures that the baked goods are easy to remove.

If you intend using the same clay pot for all types of cooking, do not cook fish as the first food in the pot. Once the pot has been used for other cooking, then it can be used for fish and seafood.

The clay pot is ideal for baking full-flavored stuffed squash.

COOKING TEMPERATURES AND TEMPERATURE CHANGES

Sudden Changes in Temperature Never expose a clay pot to any sudden changes in temperature.
● Do not place it on an electric or gas burner.
● Do not put the clay pot under the grill.
● Do not put a clay pot into a preheated oven.
● Do not turn a gas oven to the maximum required setting immediately: do this in two stages, selecting an intermediate oven temperture for the first 5 minutes' heating.
● Do not pour boiling liquid into the cold clay pot.
● Do not pour very cold liquid into the hot clay pot.
● Do not put a clay pot into the freezer.

Setting the Oven The clay pot must be placed in a cold oven and heated gradually. Set an electric oven to the required temperature as soon as the pot is placed in it. If using a gas oven, do not set it at the full temperature immediately; heat the oven in two stages by selecting a low setting for the first 5 minutes and then increasing the setting to the required temperature.

Oven Temperatures A very hot oven is generally used when cooking in a clay pot – mostly above 400F. The clay combined with the moisture from soaking act as a barrier to prevent food from burning and overcooking. The high temperature rapidly evaporates the moisture retained in the clay to produce the moist baking environ-ment within the pot.

Variations Between Ovens All settings given in the recipes are for a standard oven. If you have a forced convection oven, the cooking time will be slightly less, depending on the food. Even standard ovens vary slightly and this can be particularly noticeable when cooking food at high temperatures.

When you first cook in a clay pot, check on cooking progress about 10 minutes before the suggested cooking time, or 15 minutes if using a forced convection oven. All the recipes have been tested in a standard oven and the variation is unlikely to be very great. Once you have used the pot in your oven a few times, you will quickly become familiar with any necessary adjustments. The nature of the pot is such that food does not overcook rapidly when the lid is on. Check closely, however, when you remove the lid towards the end of the cooking time.

Adding Liquid to the Pot Never pour boiling liquid into a cold pot and do not add cold liquid to a hot pot. If the pot already has a large quantity of

hot liquid in it, for example when making a casserole, then stirring in a comparatively small amount of cold liquid will not damage it. However, do not pour cold liquid over a roast or other foods which are cooked without a significant proportion of liquid. Heat the liquid first until it is at least hand-hot.

Adapting Ordinary Recipes for Claypot Cooking The clay pot may be used for a wide variety of cooking and you will find it ideal for many of your favorite recipes. For the majority of dishes, the oven temperatures are significantly greater than those used for cooking in containers made of other materials. In some cases, the cooking times are slightly longer. However, when roasting, the higher temperature compensates to a large extent for the insulation protection provided by the clay pot.

Follow the recipes in this book when adapting your favorite dishes. For example, select one of the roast meat or poultry recipes as a guide when adding your particular choice of seasonings. There are also many basic seafood recipes, casseroles and vegetable dishes with which to compare conventional recipes.

DURING AND AFTER COOKING

Self-basting Qualities of Clay Pot Cooking Once the pot is in the oven, and the required temperature setting is reached in a gas oven, the food needs little or no attention for perfect results. The moisture from the pot ensures that the food does not dry out on the surface, acting, in some ways, as a self-basting cooking method for joints of meat or whole birds.

This enclosed, moist environment also promotes the maximum flavor permeation. By arranging the ingredients in the pot as explained in the recipes, ingredients such as herbs and spices impart the maximum flavor to the main food. Tucking herbs underneath joints, arranging a layer of ingredients in the base of the pot and placing herb sprigs or whole spices underneath or among the food all promote excellent results.

Browning and Crisping Depending on the type of food and the cooking time, there is a certain amount of browning even with the lid on the pot. However, many recipes suggest removing the lid for a short period before the end of cooking, so that roasts, baked items and gratin-style toppings develop an extra crisp texture. This final stage is very quick because of the heat of the oven.

Removing the Pot From the Oven Before removing the pot from the oven, prepare a dry wooden board or pot stand on which to place the hot pot. Alternatively, lay a thick, folded tea-towel or oven cloth on the work surface. Never place the pot on a cold or wet surface. Remember that this

The hot pot must be placed on a stand.

rule also applies to the lid, so have another suitable stand or cloth ready to hold the lid when it is removed.

Serving From the Clay Pot The clay pot makes an attractive serving dish for a variety of foods, particularly soups, gratins and casseroles. Simply add a garnish and stand the pot on a suitable heatproof mat on the table. It is a good idea to wrap a decorative cloth around the base of the pot ready for holding it when serving the food.

Any leftovers should be removed from the pot promptly and transfered to a suitable container for chilling. Cover the container and cool the food quickly, then place it in the refrigerator.

MICROWAVE COOKING

The clay pot may be used in a microwave as well as in a conventional cooker. The pot must be soaked before use. The medium and smaller size pots are both practical but the special microwave pot is ideal.

During microwave cooking, the moist clay pot absorbs some of the microwave energy so it will become hotter than some other cookware. The advantage of using the clay pot is that it moderates the cooking to promote more even results and to help in the tenderizing process when

Above: microwave pot.
Above right and below: the attractive
Romertopf apple pot.

braising meat. The clay pot helps to protect against overcooking when preparing fish and vegetables.

Always follow the microwave manufacturer's instructions. These are the best starting point for a guide to cooking times as they have been tested for the relevant appliance. When adapting microwave recipes for using a clay pot, remember that the cooking will be less rapid. The pot is usually used on a high setting (full power or 100%) but it may also be used on medium-high (about 70%) and medium (50%) settings.

At the end of the book you will find a selection of microwave recipes.

Use these as a basis for cooking similar dishes in the clay pot.

Combination Microwave Cooking
If using a combination microwave cooker, do not preheat the conventional oven. Follow the manufacturer's instructions and check the cooking progress occasionally until you are familiar with the variation in timing which results from using the clay pot.

CLEANING THE CLAY POT

In time the clay pot naturally changes color slightly to develop a patina – rather like a well-seasoned pan. Never use detergents or abrasive cleaning agents on the clay pot as

Serve a pilaf straight from the pot.

they impair the cooking qualities of the porous clay material.

Dishwashing Check the manufacturer's instructions to find out if your clay pot is dishwasher-proof. Remove any food residue by rinsing the hot pot under very hot water or by allowing it to cool, then rinsing under cold water before placing in the dishwasher.

Washing by Hand Wash the pot promptly after use in hot water with a little mild dishwashing liquid. Use a washing-up brush to scrub the inside of the pot lightly. Rinse well in clean hot water and allow to drain. Leave to dry completely before putting it away.

Removing Stubborn Baking Residue Soaking in hot water with a little mild dishwashing liquid is often sufficient to clean off any residue. However, if the pot is stained or has any baked-on residue, it should be soaked for several hours or overnight in very hot water with baking soda added to the water. This is also recommended for removing any residual flavors from the clay pot.

Another method of cleaning a heavily tainted or soiled pot (for example, if you have cooked several spicy curries or fish dishes in it and want to prepare a delicate dish) is to soak the pot for several hours or overnight. Pour off the soaking water, add cold water and baking soda with a little mild dishwashing liquid, then put the pot in the cold oven. Set the oven at 180C(350F/Gas 4) and leave for 30 minutes. Increase the oven temperature to 230C (450F/Gas 8) and leave the pot for a further 40 – 60 minutes. Allow to stand for 15 minutes. Have a kettle of boiling water ready. Scrub the inside of the pot gently, then pour away the dirty water. Rinse the pot with plenty of clean boiling water. Allow to dry.

STORING YOUR CLAY POT

After use, allow the washed clay pot to dry completely. Then invert the lid in the pot and place it in a cool dry cupboard. Do not put the lid on the pot as for cooking, and do not store the pot while it is still damp or in damp conditions. Do not seal the pot in a polythene bag. If the pot is damp when stored, not thoroughly cleaned or left in a damp place, mildew can grow on the clay. This has to be removed by soaking and baking with baking soda and water. If the pot has been out of use for some time then wash it thoroughly, particularly if it has been accidentally stored in damp or dusty conditions.

TERMS AND TECHNIQUES

The following is a guide to culinary terms and techniques used in the recipes.

Beurre Manié
This is a mixture of butter and flour which is used for thickening sauces. The flour is creamed with an equal quantity of butter to form a smooth, thick paste. The cooking juices are poured or strained into a saucepan and brought to simmering point. Small pieces of beurre manié are added to the sauce which is whisked vigorously. The butter melts and the flour combines smoothly with the juices to thicken the sauce on boiling.

Chilies, to seed
Fresh chilies vary in flavor: some are very hot while others are fairly mild with a distinctive flavor. The seeds are hot and should be removed from around the central core of pith before cooking.

Slice the stalk end off and slit the chili lengthways. Scrape out the seeds and pith, then rinse the chili well to remove any stray seeds. Wash your hands thoroughly after preparing chilies as the juices aggravate the skin – in particular, they will burn your eyes.

Clams, to clean
See Mussels.

Croûtes
A croûte is a small piece of fried bread which is cooked in the same way as croûtons. The bread is cut into squares, triangles, rounds or other decorative shapes before cooking. Croûtes may be used as a base on

which to serve food or as a garnish or accompaniment. A croûte is larger than a croûton.

Croûtons
These are small pieces of crisp-fried bread used both as a garnish and to add an interesting variation in texture to a dish. Use medium-thick slices of bread and cut off the crusts. Cut the slices into small cubes, then fry them in a mixture of butter and oil. Use a slotted spoon to toss the croûtons occasionally during cooking so that they brown evenly. When they are crisp and golden, drain the croûtons on absorbent kitchen paper.

Leeks, to clean
These can be gritty if not properly prepared. Slice the leeks and separate the slices into rings, then wash them thoroughly. Alternatively, slit the leeks in half lengthways, leaving the root end uncut, then open them out and hold under running water to wash away the dirt which is trapped in the layers of the vegetable.

Marinade
A flavoring mixture, usually with a certain amount of liquid, used for soaking food before cooking.

Marinate
To soak savory ingredients in a flavoring mixture (above) before cooking. Marinating flavors and tenderizes ingredients.

Mussels, to clean and prepare
This method is also used for clams and cockles. Thoroughly scrub the mussels in cold water, removing any

barnacles by scraping the shells with a knife. Discard any open shells which do not shut when tapped firmly. Pull away the black, hairy beard which protrudes from the shell. When the mussels are cooked, discard any shells which have not opened.

Oysters, to shuck
Shucking is the term for opening oysters. A shucking knife or oyster knife, designed for this purpose, has a short, pointed, tough blade. A short, heavy kitchen knife may be used instead. The oysters should be thoroughly scrubbed before they are opened. Have a bowl ready to catch the precious liquor which is inside the shells.

Protect your hand with a thick oven glove, then hold the oyster with the deep shell down and the flat side on top. Insert the point of the knife where the upper and lower shells are hinged, then give it a firm twist. This will break the seal between the shells. Carefully slide the knife around the oyster to detach it from the shell. Remove any bits of shell before pouring the liquor into the bowl.

Peaches, to peel
See Tomatoes.

Prove
To leave yeasted dough until doubled in size. The dough must be covered to prevent it from drying out and it must be left in a warm place. The time depends on the ingredients as well as on the room temperature. Rich and sweet doughs take longer to rise than plain doughs as the additional ingredients inhibit the yeast. Easy-blend yeasts often require only one proving whereas traditional baking yeast or ordinary dried yeast needs two proving periods. Check the manufacturer's instructions.

Standing Time
When cooking in the microwave the standing time is important as it allows the temperature to equalize within the food. During this standing time the centre of the food finishes cooking while very hot areas cool slightly.

Sweat
Vegetables are sweated when they are cooked without any fat. The clay pot is ideal for sweating vegetables in the oven. Simply mix and season the vegetables in the soaked pot: the moisture from the pot keeps the vegetables perfectly moist.

Tomatoes, to peel
Place the tomatoes in a bowl and cover with freshly boiling water. Leave to stand for 30 – 60 seconds. The less ripe the tomatoes, the longer it takes to loosen the skin. Drain and slit the skin which will peel away easily.

Single fruit may be peeled by piercing it on a metal skewer or fork and holding it over a gas flame until the skin scorches and blisters. Turn the fruit to scorch all sides, then rinse it under cold water and slide off the peel. This latter method is not suitable for peaches.

CLAM CHOWDER

16 – 24 clams, depending on size, scrubbed
lump of butter
4 rindless bacon slices, diced
2 onions, chopped
2 celery stalks, diced
3 potatoes, diced
1 garlic clove, crushed
1 bay leaf
1 sprig thyme
2 tablespoons all-purpose flour
pinch of chili powder
salt and pepper
1 cup chicken stock
1 1/2 cups milk
4 tablespoons chopped parsley
1/2 cup light cream

Place the clams in a saucepan with 1 cup water. Cover and bring to a boil. Cook, shaking occasionally, for 10 minutes, until the clams open. Remove the clams from their shells, reserving the liquor. Strain all the juices. Chop the clams. Melt the butter in the rinsed pan. Add the bacon, onions, celery, potatoes, bay leaf and thyme. Cook, stirring, for 10 minutes.

Stir in the flour, chili, salt and pepper. Pour in the reserved liquor and the stock. Add the clams and milk, stirring, and remove from the heat. Pour the mixture into the soaked clay pot, cover and place in the cold oven. Set the oven at 425F. Cook for 45 minutes, or until the potatoes are tender and the soup is well flavored. Taste for seasoning, then stir in the parsley and cream. Serve at once.

Serves 4

BEAN & SAUSAGE SOUP

$^1/_2$ pound black beans or pinto beans, soaked
    overnight
2 tablespoons oil
1 large onion, chopped
1 garlic clove, crushed
1 green chili, seeded and chopped
4 celery stalks, diced ● 1 carrot, diced
1 tablespoon ground coriander
$^1/_2$ teaspoon ground mace
pinch of ground cloves
$3^3/_4$ cups chicken stock (unsalted)
2 tablespoons tomato paste
1 pound smoked pork sausage
2 tablespoons all-purpose flour
salt and pepper
sour cream and paprika, to serve

Drain the beans. Place them in a saucepan with cold water to cover. Bring to a boil and boil rapidly for 10 minutes. Drain the beans and place in the soaked clay pot. Heat the oil. Add the onion, garlic, chili, celery and carrot, and cook for 10 minutes, until the onion is softened. Stir in the coriander, mace and cloves and cook for 2 minutes. Add the onion mixture to the beans, then pour in the stock. Cover the pot and place in the cold oven. Set the oven at 400F. Cook for 2 hours.

Meanwhile cut the sausage into chunks. Stir the flour to a paste with 3 tablespoons cold water, add a little of the hot soup, then pour the mixture into the pot. Add the sausage and tomato paste, and cook, covered, for a further 1 hour. Stir in seasoning to taste and mash some of the beans slightly. Serve topped with sour cream and paprika.

Serves 4

PEA SOUP

$^1/_2$ pound dried peas, soaked overnight
2 tablespoons oil
1 onion, chopped
2 potatoes, diced
1 bay leaf
1 sprig rosemary
1 teaspoon dried marjoram
5 cups ham or chicken stock
$1^1/_2$ cups diced cooked ham
salt and pepper
a little grated nutmeg
croûtons, to serve

Drain the peas and place them in the soaked clay pot. Heat the oil in a saucepan. Add the onion, potatoes, bay leaf and rosemary. Cook, stirring often, for 10 minutes, until the onion is softened. Stir in the marjoram.

Tip the onion mixture into the pot, then pour in the stock and stir well. Add the ham. Sprinkle in a little pepper and nutmeg but do not add salt at this stage. Cover the pot and place in the cold oven. Set the oven at 400F. Cook for 2 – 2$^1/_2$ hours, or until the peas are thoroughly tender. Taste for seasoning and sprinkle with croûtons before serving.

Serves 6

ONE-POT MINESTRONE

^{1}/2 pound cannellini beans, soaked overnight
6 rindless bacon slices, diced
1 large onion, chopped
2 garlic cloves, crushed
2 carrots, diced
2 potatoes, diced
4 cups peeled, diced tomatoes
3^1/2 cups shredded cabbage
^{1}/2 pound fava beans
1 bay leaf
2 teaspoons dried marjoram
1 tablespoon tomato paste
salt and pepper
2 tablespoons chopped parsley
^{1}/4 cup soup pasta
freshly grated Parmesan cheese, to serve

Drain the cannellini beans and place them in a saucepan with cold water to cover. Bring to the boil and boil rapidly for 10 minutes, then drain the beans and place them in the soaked clay pot. Add the bacon, onion, garlic, carrots, potatoes, tomatoes, cabbage and fava beans. Mix all these ingredients together, then add the bay leaf, marjoram and tomato paste.

Pour in 2 quarts water. Cover the pot and place in the cold oven. Set the oven at 400F. Cook for 1^1/2 hours. Stir in plenty of seasoning, the parsley and pasta and cook, covered, for a further 30 minutes, or until the pasta is tender. Taste for seasoning before serving with Parmesan cheese.

Serves 6

SPICY MULLIGATAWNY

3 tablespoons oil
2 onions, chopped
1 garlic clove, crushed
1 potato, diced
2 carrots, diced
2 tablespoons ground coriander
1 tablespoon cumin seeds
6 cardamoms
1 bay leaf
$^1/_2$ pound red lentils
salt and pepper
$5^2/_3$ cups chicken stock
4 tablespoons plain yoghurt
chopped cilantro, to garnish

Heat the oil in a saucepan. Add the onions, garlic, potato and carrots, and cook for 10 minutes, stirring all the time, until the onion is slightly softened. Stir in the coriander and cumin and cook for 2 minutes, then turn the mixture into the soaked clay pot. Add the cardamoms, bay leaf and lentils. Sprinkle in seasoning, mix well, then stir in the stock.

Cover the pot and place in the cold oven. Set the oven at 400F. Cook for $1^1/_2$ – 2 hours, stirring once. The lentils should be cooked until mushy, so that they thicken the soup, and the vegetables should be very tender. Taste for seasoning, then serve each portion topped with a little yoghurt and sprinkled with cilantro leaves.

Serves 4

LEEK & POTATO SOUP

lump of butter
1 tablespoon oil
1 pound leeks, sliced
1¹/2 pounds potatoes, diced
1 tablespoon all-purpose flour
2 cups chicken stock
salt and pepper
1 bay leaf
2 sprigs tarragon or 1 teaspoon dried tarragon
2 cups milk

Heat the butter and oil in a large saucepan. Reserve a few pieces of leek for garnish, if liked. Add the remaining leeks and potatoes, then cook, stirring, for about 5 minutes, until the leeks are slightly softened. Stir in the flour, then pour in the stock, stirring all the time.

Transfer the leek and potato mixture to the soaked clay pot. Stir in seasoning, the bay leaf and tarragon. Cover the pot and place in the cold oven. Set the oven at 400F. Cook for 50 minutes. Gradually stir the milk into the soup. Cook, covered, for a further 40 minutes, until the vegetables are tender. Serve the soup either chunky or processed until smooth in a blender. Taste for seasoning before serving, garnished with the reserved leek, if liked.

Serves 4

─HALIBUT ON VEGETABLES─

2 pounds small new potatoes
1¹/2 cups shelled fresh peas
4 small carrots, thinly sliced
4 small zucchini, trimmed and thinly sliced
6 scallions, chopped
salt and pepper
grated rind and juice of 1 lime
1¹/2 pounds halibut fillet, cut into 4 portions
1 tablespoon chopped tarragon
4 tablespoons melted butter

Cook the potatoes in boiling water for 8 –10 minutes, until almost tender. Drain and place in the soaked clay pot. Blanch the peas in boiling water for 5 minutes, drain and set aside. Blanch the carrots for 2 minutes, then add them to the potatoes. Add the zucchini, scallions, seasoning and lime rind to the vegetables in the pot. Mix well. Arrange the halibut on top of the vegetables, add a little seasoning, then sprinkle with the tarragon, lime juice and melted butter.

Cover the pot and place in the cold oven. Set the oven at 425F. Cook for 30 minutes. Add the peas, carefully arranging them between the halibut portions, then cook for a further 5 – 10 minutes, or until the halibut is cooked and the vegetables are tender.

Serves 4

CARDAMOM COD STEAKS

4 cod steaks
4 cardamoms
2 small zucchini, trimmed and grated
1 cup fresh bread crumbs
4 tablespoons snipped chives
2 tablespoons plain yoghurt
salt and pepper
2 tablespoons melted butter
lemon slices, to garnish

Cut the central bones out of the cod steaks, then lay them in the soaked clay pot. Split open each cardamom pod and carefully transfer the tiny black seeds to a mortar. Grind them to a powder using a pestle, then sprinkle the powder over the cod steaks. Mix the zucchini, bread crumbs and chives in a bowl. Stir in the yoghurt and seasoning, then divide this stuffing between the cod steaks.

Trickle the melted butter over the fish. Cover the pot and place in the cold oven. Set the oven at 425F. Cook for 35 – 40 minutes, or until the fish is cooked and the top of the stuffing is lightly browned. Serve at once, garnished with halved lemon slices, with the cooking juices poured over.

Serves 4

MARINATED TUNA WITH LIME

1 1/2 pounds tuna steak
salt and pepper
4 sprigs thyme
4 bay leaves
6 tablespoons snipped chives
grated rind and juice of 1 lime
4 tablespoons olive oil
4 tablespoons dry sherry
1 pound thin green beans, trimmed
1/2 red onion, thinly sliced
lime wedges, to garnish

Place the tuna in a dish. Season well, then top with the thyme, bay leaves and chives. Mix the lime rind and juice, olive oil and sherry in a bowl, then pour it over the fish. Cover and leave to marinate for at least 3 hours. Transfer to the soaked clay pot. Cover the pot and place in the cold oven. Set the oven at 425F. Cook for 25 minutes.

Meanwhile, add the beans to a saucepan of boiling, lightly salted water. Bring back to a boil and cook for 2 minutes. Drain. Add the beans to the pot and cook, covered, for a further 10 – 15 minutes, or until the fish is cooked through. Baste with the juices and divide between serving plates, with the beans. Add the sliced raw onion and garnish with lime wedges.

Serves 4

–MACKEREL WITH CUCUMBER–

6 large sprigs rosemary
8 mackerel fillets
salt and pepper
3 tablespoons horseradish sauce
2 gourmet cucumbers, peeled and cut into large dice
6 scallions, chopped
1 cup cider
large knob of butter
rosemary sprigs, to garnish

Lay the rosemary sprigs in the bottom of the soaked clay pot. Check that the mackerel fillets are free of bones. Season well and spread the flesh side of each fillet with a little of the horseradish sauce. Roll up the mackerel fillets from the head end and secure with wooden toothpicks. Place in the pot. Add the cucumber and scallions, then pour in the cider. Cover the pot and place in the cold oven. Set the oven at 425F. Cook for 35 – 40 minutes, or until the fish is cooked through.

Transfer the fish rolls to warmed serving plates. Use a slotted spoon to arrange the cucumber around the fish. Keep hot. Strain the juices into a saucepan and bring to a boil. Boil rapidly until reduced by half. Whisk in the butter and boil, whisking, until the butter has melted and the sauce is reduced to a flavorsome glaze. Check the seasoning, then spoon the glaze over the mackerel. Garnish with rosemary.

Serves 4

STUFFED TROUT

4 trout, cleaned with heads on
1 cup fresh bread crumbs
4 button mushrooms, chopped
4 scallions, chopped
2 tablespoons chopped parsley
2 teaspoons chopped thyme
grated rind of 1/2 lemon
salt and pepper
2 tablespoons dry sherry
2 tablespoons slivered almonds
4 tablespoons melted butter
lemon wedges, to serve
parsley sprigs, to garnish

Rinse the trout and dry them on paper towels. Mix together the bread crumbs, mushrooms, scallions, parsley, thyme and lemon rind. Add seasoning and stir in the sherry to bind this stuffing. Use a teaspoon to divide the stuffing between the fish, pressing it into the body cavities.

Lay the trout in the soaked clay pot. Sprinkle with the almonds, then trickle the melted butter all over the top. Cover the pot and place in the cold oven. Set the oven at 425F. Cook for 35 – 45 minutes, until the almonds are browned and the fish is cooked through. Test by piercing the thick part of one fish with the point of a knife. Serve with lemon wedges and garnish with parsley.

Serves 4

-DILL-CREAM SALMON STEAKS-

4 bay leaves
4 scallions, chopped
4 salmon steaks
4 tablespoons chopped dill
2 teaspoons superfine sugar
salt and pepper
2 tablespoons lemon juice
4 tablespoons melted butter
1 cup sour cream
dill sprigs, to garnish

Lay the bay leaves in the soaked clay pot. Sprinkle half the scallions over, then arrange the salmon steaks on top. Sprinkle half the dill, the remaining scallions, the sugar and seasoning evenly over the fish. Trickle the lemon juice over, then do the same with the melted butter. Cover the pot and place in the cold oven. Set the oven at 425F. Cook for 30 – 35 minutes, or until the salmon is cooked.

Meanwhile, stir the remaining chopped dill into the sour cream. Use a fish slice to transfer the fish carefully to warmed plates. The bay leaves may be reserved for garnishing. Stir the cooking juices into the dill cream and taste for seasoning. Pour a little dill cream over each salmon steak and offer the rest separately. Garnish with dill and bay, if liked. Serve at once, with new potatoes and salad.

Serves 4

—SPICED FISH WITH SPINACH—

1 pound spinach, trimmed
1/4 cup butter or margarine
2 garlic cloves
3 tablespoons grated fresh ginger root
1 tablespoon cumin seeds
4 cardamoms
1 tablespoon ground coriander
1 teaspoon ground turmeric
2 tablespoons plain yoghurt
salt and pepper
1/2 pound peeled, cooked shrimp
8 fine white fish fillets, skinned
4 tomatoes, peeled and chopped
1 tablespoon chopped cilantro
lemon wedges, to garnish

Wash the spinach, then put the wet leaves in a large saucepan. Cover and cook over high heat, shaking the pan often, for about 5 minutes, or until the leaves have shrunk. Drain well, then place the spinach in the soaked clay pot. Melt the butter or margarine in the pan. Add the garlic and ginger root, and cook for 3 minutes, stirring, then add the cumin, cardamoms, coriander and turmeric and cook for a further 2 minutes. Remove from the heat and stir in the yoghurt and plenty of seasoning.

Spread the shrimp out over the spinach. Arrange the fish fillets over the top, then spoon the spice mixture over. Cover the pot and place in the cold oven. Set the oven at 425F. Cook for 40 minutes, or until the fish is just firm. Top with the tomatoes and sprinkle with the chopped cilantro, then serve garnished with lemon wedges. Basmati rice or nan bread are ideal accompaniments.

Serves 4

OYSTERS ROCKEFELLER

large lump of butter
2 tablespoons finely chopped onion
2 tablespoons chopped celery leaves
1 pound fresh spinach, shredded
salt and pepper
24 oysters, opened and liquor reserved
2 tablespoons chopped parsley
1 cup fresh bread crumbs
3 tablespoons light cream
1 tablespoon Pastis, Pernod or other aniseed liqueur
dash of Tabasco sauce

Melt the butter in a large saucepan. Add the onion, celery leaves and spinach. Cook, stirring, until the spinach wilts, then continue to cook over a fairly high heat for about 10 minutes, or until the excess moisture has evaporated. Reduce the heat. Stir in seasoning and the liquor from the oysters. Add the parsley and half the bread crumbs. Spoon the mixture into the soaked clay pot and spread it out evenly.

Arrange the oysters on the spinach. Mix the cream, aniseed liqueur and the smallest dash of Tabasco sauce, then trickle this mixture over the oysters. Sprinkle with the remaining bread crumbs. Cover the pot and place in the cold oven. Set the oven at 425F. Cook for 35 minutes. Serve at once.

Serves 4 – 6

—MUSSELS WITH MUSHROOMS—

2 pounds mussels
1/4 cup butter
1 small onion, finely chopped
1 garlic clove, crushed
grated rind of 1 lemon
3/4 pound mushrooms, sliced
1 cup dry white wine
salt and pepper
4 tablespoons chopped dill

Scrub the mussels and pull off the feathery black beards which protrude from the shells. Discard any open mussels which do not shut when tapped. Place in the soaked clay pot. Melt the butter in a large saucepan. Add the onion and garlic, and cook for 5 minutes. Stir in the lemon rind and mushrooms, then cook for 15 minutes, until the mushrooms are greatly reduced and a good deal of the liquid has evaporated. Stir in the wine and seasoning, and bring to a boil.

Ladle the mushroom mixture over the mussels. Cover the pot and place in the cold oven. Set the oven at 425F. Cook for 20 minutes. Hold the pot lid firmly and give the mussels a good shake. Cook, covered, for a further 15 minutes, until all the mussels are open. Ladle the mussels and their juices into warmed bowls, discarding any unopened shells, sprinkle with the chopped dill and serve at once with crusty bread.

Serves 4

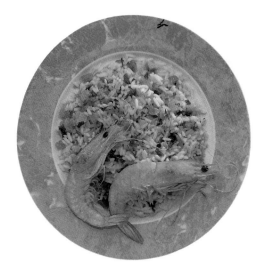

JAMBALAYA

1 large onion, chopped
1 green sweet pepper, seeded and diced
1 garlic clove, crushed
$^1/_4$ – $^1/_2$ teaspoon chili powder
1 teaspoon dried oregano
1 bay leaf
$1^1/_2$ cups long-grain rice
3 cups diced cooked ham
4 tomatoes, peeled and diced
$3^3/_4$ cups chicken stock
salt and pepper
2 tablespoons chopped parsley
12 large shrimp

Place the onion, green sweet pepper, garlic, chili powder, oregano and bay leaf in the soaked clay pot. Add the rice, ham and tomatoes, and mix well, then pour in the stock. Sprinkle in a little seasoning. Cover the pot and place in the cold oven. Set the oven at 425F. Cook for 30 minutes. Stir the mixture, then cook, covered, for a further 30 minutes.

Sprinkle the parsley over the rice, then arrange the shrimp on top. Cook, covered, for a further 15 minutes, or until the shrimp are heated. Serve with a crisp green salad and crusty bread.

Serves 4

SEAFOOD WITH FENNEL

1/4 cup butter
2 tablespoons olive oil
1 onion, sliced
2 bulbs fennel, sliced
salt and pepper
1 can (28 - ounce) chopped tomatoes
1/2 pound peeled, cooked shrimp
1/2 pound shelled, cooked mussels
8 shelled, raw scallops
1 pound white fish fillet, skinned and cut in
   chunks
10 black olives, pitted and sliced
4 large sprigs basil, shredded
freshly grated Parmesan cheese, to serve

Melt the butter with the oil in a saucepan. Add the onion and fennel. Sprinkle in plenty of seasoning and cook, stirring often, for 20 minutes, or until the onion and fennel are softened. Stir in the tomatoes and bring to a boil. Simmer for 3 minutes, then turn the mixture into the soaked clay pot.

Mix the shrimp, mussels and scallops into the tomato and fennel mixture in the pot. Add the white fish, distributing the chunks on the surface of the tomato mixture. Cover the pot and place in the cold oven. Set the oven at 425F. Cook for 35 minutes, or until the fish is cooked. Taste for seasoning, then combine the fish gently with the fennel and sauce, adding the olives and basil. Serve at once, with Parmesan cheese and rice, pasta or chunks of crusty bread.

Serves 4

——— FISHERMAN'S FAVORITE ———

1¹/2 pounds white fish fillet, skinned and cut into
    chunks
grated rind and juice of 1 lemon
salt and pepper
¹/2 pound mushrooms, sliced
4 tablespoons chopped parsley
4 scallions, chopped
1¹/2 cups grated cheese
4 tablespoons cider or dry white wine
¹/2 cup cream cheese
2 pounds potatoes, cooked and sliced
lump of butter

Lay half the fish in the soaked clay pot. Top
with half the lemon rind and juice and
season well. Add half the mushrooms, parsley
and scallions, then sprinkle about a third of
the grated cheese over. Repeat the layers
once more. Pour the cider or wine over the
ingredients and dot the cream cheese evenly
over the top. Finally, cover with a layer of
potato, overlapping the slices neatly.
Sprinkle the remaining grated cheese over
and dot with butter.

Cover the pot and place in the cold oven.
Set the oven at 425F. Cook for 35 minutes.
Uncover the pot and cook for a further 15
minutes, or until the potato topping is well
browned and the layers of fish are cooked
through. Serve piping hot.

Serves 4

PILAF-STUFFED CHICKEN

2 tablespoons olive oil
1 garlic clove, crushed
1 onion, chopped
4 tablespoons raisins
2 teaspoons chopped oregano
4 tablespoons pine nuts or cashew nuts
1 cinnamon stick
4 cloves
3/4 cup long-grain rice
1 cup chicken stock
salt and pepper
3 1/2- pound chicken
4 bay leaves
4 sprigs thyme
4 tablespoons sweet sherry

Heat the oil in a saucepan. Add the garlic, onion, raisins, oregano, pine or cashew nuts, cinnamon stick and cloves. Cook, stirring gently, for 5 minutes. Stir in the rice and pour in the stock. Bring to a boil, cover the pan and simmer for 15 minutes. Meanwhile, thoroughly rinse and dry the chicken with paper towels. Spoon the rice mixture into the body cavity, with any moisture from the pan. Tie the ends of the chicken legs together neatly.

Place the chicken in the soaked clay pot. Tuck the bay leaves and thyme sprigs in and around the chicken, then season it well all over. Cover the pot and place in the cold oven. Set the oven at 425F. Cook for 1 hour. Brush the sweet sherry all over the chicken and cook for a further 15 minutes, or until the chicken is cooked through and golden.

Serves 4

CHICKEN BOULANGERE

1 lemon, sliced
2 bay leaves
2 pounds potatoes, sliced
1 large onion, thinly sliced
4 tablespoons chopped tarragon
salt and pepper
2 tablespoons melted butter
4 chicken quarters

Lay half the lemon slices in the bottom of the soaked clay pot. Add the bay leaves, then layer the potatoes and onion on top. Sprinkle half the tarragon and plenty of seasoning over the vegetables. Trickle half the melted butter over. Arrange the chicken quarters on top of the vegetables. Season them well and sprinkle with the remaining tarragon. Trickle the rest of the melted butter over the chicken quarters, then tuck the remaining lemon slices around them.

Cover the pot and place in the cold oven. Set the oven at 425F. Cook for 40 minutes. Uncover the pot and cook for a further 15 – 20 minutes, or until the chicken quarters are cooked through, crisp and golden. The vegetables should be tender. Serve the chicken with the vegetables, discarding the lemon slices, which are included for flavour, or using them as a garnish. Serve with seasonal vegetables.

Serves 4

—CHICKEN WITH BROCCOLI—

8 chicken thighs
2 tablespoons all-purpose flour
salt and pepper
2 tablespoons oil
1 teaspoon chopped thyme or $1/2$ teaspoon dried
   thyme
1 tablespoon chopped sage or $1 1/2$ teaspoons dried sage
1 cup dry white wine
1 pound broccoli
$1/2$ cup sour cream

Dust the chicken thighs all over with the flour and plenty of seasoning. Heat the oil in a skillet. Brown the chicken pieces all over, then transfer to the soaked clay pot. Add any remaining flour to the pan juices, stir in the thyme and sage, then pour in the wine. Pour this sauce over the chicken. Cover the pot and place in the cold oven. Set the oven at 425F. Cook for 30 minutes.

Meanwhile, blanch the broccoli stems in boiling salted water for 3 minutes, drain well. Add the stems to the pot, tucking them between the chicken, and baste with the sauce. Cook, covered, for a further 15 minutes, or until the chicken is thoroughly cooked. Transfer the chicken and broccoli to warmed serving plates. Stir the sour cream into the sauce, check the seasoning, then spoon it over the chicken.

Serves 4

BEGGAR'S CHICKEN

8 chicken drumsticks or thighs
1 teaspoon sesame oil
1 tablespoon dry sherry
$^1/_4$ teaspoon five-spice powder
$^1/_4$ teaspoon ground white pepper
1 garlic clove, crushed
1 teaspoons grated fresh ginger root
4 tablespoons soy sauce
2 tablespoons sesame seeds
8 scallions, to garnish

Make two or three slits into the meat on each chicken piece, then place them in a dish. Mix together the oil, sherry, five-spice powder, pepper, garlic, ginger root and soy sauce, then brush the mixture all over the chicken pieces. Cover and chill for at least 5 hours, or preferably overnight. Meanwhile, trim the scallions and cut the green part into fine strips, all attached at the root end. Place in iced water for at least 30 minutes so that the strips curl.

Transfer the chicken to the soaked clay pot with all the marinating juices. Cover the pot and place in the cold oven. Set the oven at 475F. Cook for 35 minutes. Baste the chicken well with the cooking juices and sprinkle with the sesame seeds. Cook, uncovered, for a further 15 minutes. Serve piping hot, with cooked rice, garnished with the scallion curls.

Serves 4

COQ AU VIN

4 chicken quarters, skinned
1 garlic clove, crushed
1 bouquet garni
salt and pepper
1 bottle red wine
$^1/_4$ cup butter
1 tablespoon olive oil
4 rindless bacon slices, diced
$^3/_4$ pound pearl onions, halved if large
3 tablespoons all-purpose flour
$^3/_4$ pound button mushrooms
4 tablespoons chopped parsley
parsley sprigs and croûtons, to garnish

Place the chicken quarters in a bowl. Add the garlic, bouquet garni, plenty of seasoning and the wine. Cover and chill for 24 hours. Heat half the butter and the oil in a skillet. Lift the chicken from the bowl, pat dry, then brown the portions all over. Place in the soaked clay pot. Fry the bacon and onions until the onions are lightly browned. Add to the chicken with the marinade. Cover the pot and place in the cold oven. Set the oven at 425F. Cook for 45 minutes.

Add the mushrooms to the pot and cook for a further 45 minutes, until the chicken is tender and cooked. Meanwhile, cream the remaining butter with the flour. Pour the sauce into a saucepan and transfer the chicken to warmed plates. Boil the sauce, then whisk in knobs of the butter and flour mixture. Boil, whisking for 3 minutes. Ladle the sauce over the chicken, sprinkle generously with parsley and garnish with croûtons.

Serves 4

—SWEET 'N' SPICY GAME HENS—

$^1/_3$ cup wild rice
salt and pepper
$^1/_3$ cup long-grain rice
1 small onion, chopped
grated rind and juice of 1 orange
4 x 1-pound Cornish game hens
2 tablespoons melted butter
2 tablespoons clear honey
$^1/_4$ teaspoon turmeric
$^1/_2$ teaspoon ground ginger
1 teaspoon ground coriander
4 tablespoons slivered almonds
1 cup Greek-style yoghurt
2-inch piece English cucumber, grated
1 teaspoon chopped mint

Cook the wild rice in boiling salted water for 30 minutes. Drain. Simmer the long-grain rice and onion in a covered saucepan with $^1/_2$ cup water for 20 minutes. Mix both types of rice. Add the grated orange rind and seasoning. Spoon the rice into the body cavities of the Cornish game hens, then place them in the soaked clay pot. Mix the butter, honey, turmeric, ginger and coriander.

Brush the butter mixture all over the Cornish game hens and season well. Cover the pot and place in the cold oven. Set at 400F. Cook for 45 minutes. Sprinkle the birds with the almonds. Cook, covered, for a further 25 – 30 minutes, until the birds are golden and cooked through. Mix together the yoghurt, cucumber and mint and offer with the birds.

Serves 4

— CHICKEN WITH EGGPLANTS —

2 large eggplants, sliced
salt and pepper
^{1}/4 cup butter
1 onion, sliced
1 tablespoon ground coriander
8 thyme sprigs
5 oranges
grated nutmeg
4 chicken quarters

Place the eggplant slices in a strainer, sprinkling each layer with salt. Set aside over a bowl for 30 minutes. Rinse and pat dry, then place in the soaked clay pot. Melt half the butter in a skillet, add the onion and cook for 3 minutes. Sprinkle the coriander over the eggplants, then spread the onion slices on top and pour the cooking juices over. Place the chicken quarters in the pot, tucking a thyme sprig under each one.

Grate the rind and squeeze the juice from 1 orange. Sprinkle nutmeg and seasoning over the chicken quarters. Cover the pot and place in the cold oven. Set the oven at 425F. Cook for 40 minutes. Cut all the peel and pith from the remaining oranges, then slice them, discarding the seeds. Arrange around the chicken and dot with the remaining butter. Cook, covered, for a further 15 – 20 minutes. Serve garnished with the remaining thyme sprigs.

Serves 4

FESTIVE CHICKEN

4 boneless chicken breasts, skinned
salt and pepper
$^1/_2$ teaspoon ground mace
large lump of butter
$^1/_4$ pound pearl onions, halved
1 tablespoon all-purpose flour
4 tablespoons brandy
1 cup dry white wine
$^1/_2$ pound ready-to-eat dried apricots, halved
$^1/_4$ pound ready-to-eat dried prunes, halved
4 bay leaves
$^1/_4$ pound small button mushrooms

Make two or three small cuts across each chicken breast, then season well and sprinkle with mace. Melt the butter in a skillet and brown the chicken, then put in the soaked clay pot. Brown the onions in the butter in the skillet, then transfer them to the pot.

Stir the flour into the remaining fat. Pour in the brandy and wine, then bring to a boil, stirring. Add the apricots, prunes, bay leaves and mushrooms. Stir well, then pour the mixture over the chicken. Cover the pot and place in the cold oven. Set the oven at 425F. Cook for 50 minutes, or until the chicken is cooked through. Taste the sauce for seasoning and serve.

Serves 4

CHICKEN CHEERIO

8 chicken thighs
1 tablespoon cornstarch
salt and pepper
1 teaspoon ground ginger
2 cans (14-ounce) chick peas
1 can (14-ounce) artichoke hearts, drained
grated rind and juice of 1 lemon
6 cardamoms
4 bay leaves
1/2 cup chicken stock
1 tablespoon pistachio or walnut oil
2 tablespoons sunflower oil

Dust the chicken with the cornstarch, seasoning and the ginger. Tip the chick peas and the can liquid into the soaked clay pot. Mix in the artichoke hearts. Arrange the chicken pieces on top, then sprinkle the lemon rind and juice over.

Add the cardamoms and bay leaves. Pour in the stock. Trickle the pistachio or walnut oil over the chicken first, then top with the sunflower oil. Cover the pot and place in the cold oven. Set the oven at 450F. Cook for 50 – 55 minutes, until the chicken thighs are well cooked. Serve at once.

Serves 4

TURKEY ROULADES

4 thin turkey breast fillets
6 tablespoons fresh bread crumbs
4 tablespoons chopped cooked ham
4 scallions, chopped
2 tablespoons chopped parsley
1 tablespoon chopped sage or 1 teaspoon dried sage
salt and pepper
3 tablespoons milk
6 – 8 tablespoons cranberry sauce
3 tablespoons all-purpose flour
1 tablespoon oil
1 cup cider
4 tablespoons sour cream
fresh herbs, to garnish

Place the turkey meat between two sheets of waxed paper and beat them out thinly, if necessary, with a rolling pin. Mix together the bread crumbs, ham, scallions, parsley, sage and seasoning. Stir in the milk to bind the mixture, then spread it thinly over the turkey. Spread some cranberry sauce thinly over the bread crumb mixture, then roll up the turkey fillets. Secure with wooden toothpicks. Dust all over with flour and seasoning.

Heat the oil in a skillet, brown the roulades, then put in the soaked clay pot. Add any remaining flour to the pan and stir in the cider. Season, then pour the sauce over the roulades. Cover the pot and place in the cold oven. Set the oven at 450F. Cook for 50 minutes. Remove the toothpicks, slice and fan out the roulades. Stir the cream into the sauce and garnish with herbs before serving. Offer with salad or seasonal vegetables.

Serves 4

ROAST TURKEY

oven-ready turkey weighing up to 10 pounds
2 fresh bouquets garnis
2 onions
salt and pepper
6 rindless bacon slices
4 tablespoons all-purpose flour
2 cups giblet stock (see method)

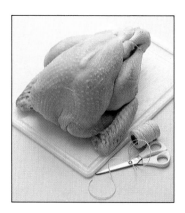

Weigh, rinse and thoroughly dry the turkey. Place one bouquet garni and one onion in the body cavity, then truss the bird neatly. Slice the remaining onion and lay the slices in the soaked clay pot. Place the bird on top and add the remaining bouquet garni. Lay the bacon over the turkey. Cover the pot and place in the cold oven. Set the oven at 400F. Cook for 20 minutes per pound plus an extra 20 minutes.

Giblet stock is made by boiling the turkey giblets with a sliced onion, carrot and bay leaf in water to cover for 1 hour. Strain. Skim the fat from the turkey cooking juices, then pour them into a saucepan. Stir in the flour and cook, stirring for 10 – 15 minutes, or until lightly browned. Stir in the stock and bring to a boil. Simmer for 2 minutes, season and serve with the carved turkey.

Serves 12 – 14

STUFFINGS FOR TURKEY

Pack one of the stuffings under the skin covering the breast meat. Loosen the skin first with a knife, then push a spoon between it and the flesh. Simply mix together all the given ingredients.

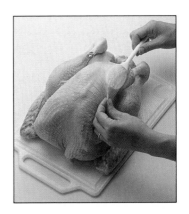

CHESTNUT STUFFING
1 pound chestnuts, cooked, peeled and chopped
1 large onion, finely chopped
1 cup fresh bread crumbs
2 tablespoons chopped parsley
2 tablespoons chopped sage or 1 tablespoon dried sage
1^1/2 cups diced cooked ham
salt and pepper
milk, to bind

SAUSAGEMEAT STUFFING
1 pound pork sausagemeat
2 tablespoons chopped parsley
1 cup fresh bread crumbs
1 small onion, finely chopped
1 tablespoon chopped thyme or 1^1/2 teaspoons dried
    thyme
salt and pepper
4 tablespoons red wine

GAME-STYLE STUFFING
1 onion, finely chopped
^{1}/2 pound ground pork
^{3}/4 cup chopped mushrooms
2 cups fresh bread crumbs
^{1}/2 teaspoon ground mace
6 juniper berries, crushed
3 tablespoons chopped parsley
2 tablespoons raisins, chopped
4 – 6 tablespoons port, to bind

Any surplus stuffing may be rolled into balls and added to the pot about 1 hour before the turkey is cooked.

TURKEY WITH PEPPERS

1 pound uncooked boneless turkey breast, cut in
   chunks
2 tablespoons all-purpose flour
salt and pepper
3 tablespoons olive oil
1 garlic clove, crushed
1 onion, halved and sliced
1 green sweet pepper, seeded and thinly sliced
1 red sweet pepper, seeded and thinly sliced
1 teaspoon dried marjoram
8 plum tomatoes, chopped
1 cup red wine
12 black olives, pitted and sliced
handful of basil leaves
8 tacos shells, to serve (optional)
$^{1}/_{2}$ cup sour cream

Coat the turkey with the flour and plenty of
seasoning and place in the soaked clay pot.
Heat the oil in a skillet. Add the garlic,
onion and peppers and cook for 5 minutes,
then pour the mixture over the turkey. Top
with the marjoram and tomatoes, then pour
in the wine. Cover the pot and place in
the cold oven. Set the oven at 450F. Cook
for 50 minutes, stirring the mixture once, or
until the turkey is well cooked.

Stir in the olives. Reserve some basil for
garnish, if liked, then use scissors to shred the
remaining leaves and soft stems. Mix the
shredded basil into the turkey mixture and
taste for seasoning. The mixture may be
served in tacos shells. Heat the shells on a
baking sheet in the oven for 2 – 3 minutes
before the turkey is cooked. Spoon the
mixture into the shells. Spoon a little sour
cream over the turkey and garnish with basil,
if liked. Serve at once.

Serves 4

DUCK A L'ORANGE

1 5-pound duck
1 onion
4 cloves
2 large oranges
4 bay leaves
1 sprig rosemary
salt and pepper
1 cup dry white wine
4 tablespoons orange liqueur
2 tablespoons granulated sugar
2 teaspoons cornstarch

Rinse and dry the duck on paper towels. Prick the skin all over. Stick the onion with the cloves, then place in the body cavity of the duck. Squeeze and reserve the juice from 1 orange, then place the two shells in the body cavity. Place the duck in the soaked clay pot. Add the bay leaves and rosemary sprig, then season the duck well all over. Cover the pot and place in the cold oven. Set the oven at 475F. Cook for 1¹/₂ hours, or until the duck is tender.

Skim the fat from the cooking juices, then pour them into a saucepan. Return the pot, uncovered, for 10 minutes to the oven to crisp the duck. Add the reserved orange juice to the pan with the grated rind and juice of the remaining orange, the wine, liqueur and sugar and boil for 5 minutes. Blend the cornstarch with a little water, stir in some of the hot sauce, then return to the pan and bring to a boil. Remove from the heat at once. Serve with the carved duck.

Serves 4

DUCK WITH BABY CORN

4 boneless duck breasts
2 tablespoons oil
2 teaspoons walnut or pistachio oil
salt and pepper
1 teaspoon paprika
2 tablespoons chopped mixed herbs
1/2 pound baby corn cobs
1/4 pound snow peas
1 small leek, white part only, sliced
4 tablespoons dry sherry
4 tablespoons shelled pistachio nuts
herb sprigs, to garnish

Prick the skin on the duck portions, then place them in the soaked clay pot. Sprinkle with both oils, salt and pepper, paprika and herbs. Cover the pot and place in the cold oven. Set at 450F. Cook for 40 minutes. Meanwhile, add the corn cobs to a small saucepan of boiling water and boil for 3 minutes. Add the leeks and cook for 1 minute, then add the snow peas, shake the pan and drain at once. Set aside.

Remove the duck from the pot. Tip in all the vegetables, toss them in the cooking juices, then replace the duck on top. Sprinkle the sherry over and top the duck with the nuts. Return the pot, uncovered, to the oven and cook for a further 15 minutes. Garnish with herb sprigs and serve at once, with fresh noodles, couscous or a mixture of wild rice and Basmati rice.

Serves 4

–GARLIC DUCK WITH LENTILS–

2 garlic heads
4 duck quarters
grated rind and juice of 1 lime
6 tablespoons chopped parsley
4 savory or thyme sprigs
2 blades of mace
1 cinnamon stick
salt and pepper
$^3/4$ pound green lentils
1 large onion, chopped
2 tablespoons all-purpose flour
1 cup chicken stock

Peel the garlic cloves. Place in a small saucepan and pour in water to cover. Bring to a boil, reduce the heat and cover the pan. Simmer for 20 minutes, then drain. Prick the duck pieces, place them in the soaked clay pot and add the garlic cloves around them. Sprinkle with the lime rind and juice and parsley. Add the thyme, mace and cinnamon, tucking them under the duck. Season well. Cover the pot and place in the cold oven. Set at 425F. Cook for 40 minutes.

Meanwhile, place the lentils in a saucepan with water to cover. Add the onion and bring to a boil. Reduce the heat, cover and simmer for 30 minutes. Drain. Drain the cooking juices from the duck into a saucepan. Stir in the flour and heat, then add the stock and bring to a boil, stirring, and add seasoning. Set the duck pieces aside, tip the lentils into the pot, then replace the duck on top. Pour in the sauce. Return the pot, uncovered, to the oven for a further 15 minutes.

Serves 4

SALT BEEF SPECIAL

1 large onion, sliced
4-pound piece rolled salt beef or beef brisket
salt and pepper
1 tablespoon pickling spice
1 cup red wine
4 bay leaves
4 sprigs parsley
1 small green cabbage, cut in wedges
6 carrots, sliced
6 large potatoes, halved

Separate the onion slices into rings and spread them over the bottom of the soaked clay pot. Place the chosen cut of beef on top. If using brisket, sprinkle with salt. Add pepper and the pickling spice, then pour in the wine and 1/2 cup water. Add the bay leaves and parsley sprigs, tucking them around the meat.

Cover the pot and place in the cold oven. Set the oven at 450F. Cook for 1 1/2 hours. Arrange the cabbage, carrots and potatoes in the pot. Pour in 1/2 cup hot water. Cook, covered, for a further 1 hour, until the meat is cooked through and the vegetables are tender. Transfer the meat and vegetables to a serving platter. Carve the meat into thick slices to serve. Offer the cooking juices separately.

Serves 6

POT ROAST

3-pound chuck steak in one piece
salt and pepper
2 large onions, thickly sliced
4 carrots, thickly sliced
2 parsnips, thickly sliced
$1/2$ teaspoon ground mace
1 bouquet garni
4 rindless bacon slices
2 cups stout
6 large potatoes, quartered

Tie the meat into a neat shape, then season it well all over. Sprinkle the onions over the base of the soaked clay pot. Top with a layer of carrots and another of parsnips. Add the mace and bouquet garni, then place the meat on top of the herbs. Cover the meat with the bacon slices and pour in the stout. Add 1 cup water. Cover the pot and place in the cold oven. Set the oven at 450F. Cook for $1^{1}/2$ hours.

Baste the meat well and add the potatoes to the pot, arranging them around the meat. Cook for a further 45 minutes until the potatoes are tender and the meat is cooked through. Transfer the meat to a serving plate with the vegetables. Strain the cooking liquid into a sauceboat and serve separately.

Serves 6

BRISKET WITH JUNIPER

3-pound boned and rolled beef brisket
2 tablespoons all-purpose flour
10 juniper berries, crushed
1 teaspoon chopped rosemary
1 teaspoon chopped thyme
1 teaspoon grated nutmeg
salt and pepper
2 teaspoons cider vinegar
1 tablespoon brown sugar
2 pounds pearl onions
1 pound small mushrooms
1 cup red wine

Make sure the meat is trimmed of excess fat and neatly tied, then place it in the soaked clay pot. Mix together the flour, juniper berries, rosemary, thyme, nutmeg and plenty of seasoning. Add the cider vinegar and brown sugar. Rub this seasoning mixture all over the meat. Pour the red wine into the bottom of the pot and add 1 cup water. Add the onions. Cover the pot and place in the cold oven. Set the oven at 450F. Cook for 2 hours.

Baste the meat and add the mushrooms, and cook, covered, for a further 1¹/4 hours, until the meat is succulent and tender. Serve with boiled or mashed potatoes, rice or pasta.

Serves 6

GERMAN SAUERBRATEN

10 cloves
1 bouquet garni
2 bay leaves
4 juniper berries, crushed
6 peppercorns, crushed
3 garlic cloves, crushed
1 onion, sliced
salt
1 cup red wine vinegar
4-pound rolled rump of beef
$^{1}/_{4}$ cup butter
4 rindless bacon slices, diced
1 cup red wine
3 tablespoons soft brown sugar
4 tablespoons raisins
2 tablespoons all-purpose flour

Place the cloves, bouquet garni, bay leaves, juniper berries, peppercorns, garlic, onion and a sprinkling of salt in a saucepan. Add the vinegar and 1 cup water and bring to a boil. Set aside to cool. Place the beef in a large bowl and pour the vinegar mixture over. Cover and chill to marinate for 2 days, turning the meat often and basting with the marinade. Drain the meat, reserving the marinade. Heat half the butter in a skillet. Add the bacon and the beef, then brown the meat.

Transfer the meat and bacon to the soaked clay pot. Boil the marinade until reduced by half, leave to cool, strain over the meat and add the wine, sugar and raisins. Cover the pot and place in the cold oven. Set the oven at 450F. Cook for 2$^{1}/_{2}$ hours. Mix the remaining butter and flour to a paste. Simmer the sauce in a saucepan, whisking in the paste. Cook for 3 minutes, then pour over the sliced beef.

Serves 6

BOEUF BOURGUIGNONNE

2 pounds braising steak, cubed
1 bouquet garni
2 garlic cloves, crushed
salt and pepper
1 bottle red wine
$^1/4$ cup butter
1 tablespoon oil
4 rindless bacon slices, diced
$^3/4$ pound pearl onions
4 tablespoons brandy
$^1/2$ pound small mushrooms
3 tablespoons all-purpose flour
3 tablespoons chopped parsley
herb sprigs and croûtons, to garnish

Place the steak in a bowl. Add the bouquet garni, garlic and seasoning, then pour in the wine. Cover and chill for 24 hours. Drain the meat, reserving the marinade. Heat half the butter and oil, brown the bacon and onions, then transfer to the soaked clay pot. Brown the meat, pour in the brandy and set it alight. When the flames subside, pour the meat and juices into the pot. Add the marinade.

Cover the pot and place in the cold oven. Set the oven at 450F. Cook for 2 hours. Mix the remaining butter and flour to a paste. Gradually whisk this into the meat mixture. Add the mushrooms. Cook, covered, for a further 30 minutes. Taste for seasoning. Sprinkle with chopped parsley and garnish with croûtons. Serve with noodles and a crisp green salad.

Serves 4 – 6

BEEF CHUKA-CHUKA

1 pound braising steak, finely diced
1 green chili, seeded and chopped
2 garlic cloves, crushed
$1/4$ teaspoon ground allspice
$1/2$ teaspoon ground ginger
4 tablespoons raisins
2 large onions, finely chopped
juice of $1/2$ lemon
2 tablespoons mango chutney, chopped
salt and pepper
$1^1/2$ pounds sweet potato, diced
1 firm mango, peeled and diced
1 tablespoon chopped mint
1 Iceberg or romaine lettuce

Place the beef in a bowl. Add the chili, garlic, allspice, ginger, raisins, onions, lemon juice and mango chutney. Sprinkle in seasoning, mix thoroughly and leave to marinate for at least 1 hour. The mixture may be chilled overnight. Turn it into the soaked clay pot and add 1 cup water. Cover the pot and place in the cold oven. Set the oven at 425F. Cook for 30 minutes.

Stir in the sweet potato and cook, covered, for a further 30 minutes. Finally, add the mango and cook, covered, for another 30 minutes, until the meat is really succulent. The mixture should be juicy, neither watery nor too dry, so add a little extra hot water if necessary. Mix in the mint lightly before serving. The mixture is eaten by spooning some on to a lettuce leaf, folding the leaf and munching through the package.

Serves 4 – 6

BEEF DOPIAZA

2 pounds lean stewing beef, cubed
2 tablespoons ground coriander
1 teaspoon ground cumin
1/2 teaspoon chili powder (optional)
salt and pepper
4 tablespoons oil
1 pound onions, thinly sliced
1 cup plain yoghurt
4 garlic cloves
4 tablespoons grated fresh ginger root
1 cinnamon stick
4 cloves
6 cardamoms
2 tablespoons chopped cilantro
lemon wedges, to serve

Place the beef in a bowl. Add the coriander, cumin, chili (if used) and plenty of seasoning. Toss the beef to coat it in the spices and set aside. Heat half the oil in a skillet. Add two-thirds of the onions and fry until golden brown. Meanwhile, purée the remaining oil and onions with the yoghurt, garlic and ginger root. Pour this paste over the meat, add the cinnamon, cloves and cardamoms and mix well.

Reserve some of the browned onion for garnish. Layer the rest of the onions and the meat mixture in the soaked clay pot. Cover the pot and place in the cold oven. Set the oven at 400F. Cook for 2¹/₂ hours, until the meat is tender. Taste for seasoning, then sprinkle the reserved onions over the dopiaza and cook, uncovered, for 10 minutes. Serve garnished with the reserved browned onion and the chopped cilantro. Offer lemon wedges for their juice.

Serves 4 – 6

SHEPPARDS PIE

1 tablespoon oil
1 large onion, chopped
1 pound ground beef
1 carrot, diced
1/4 pound mushrooms, sliced
1 teaspoon dried mixed herbs
salt and pepper
2 tablespoons all-purpose flour
1 1/2 cups beef stock
1 1/2 pounds potatoes, boiled and mashed
lump of butter
parsley sprigs, to garnish (optional)

Heat the oil in a large pan. Add the onion and cook for 5 minutes, then stir in the meat and cook until lightly browned. Add the carrot, mushrooms, herbs and seasoning. Stir in the flour, then pour in the stock, stirring. Turn the meat mixture into the soaked clay pot.

Cover the meat mixture with the mashed potatoes and mark the top with a fork. Dot with butter. Cover the pot and place in the cold oven. Set the oven at 450F. Cook for 30 minutes. Uncover the pot and cook for a further 15 minutes. Serve piping hot, garnished with parsley if liked.

Serves 4

TORTILLA TOPPER

2 tablespoons oil
2 onions, halved and sliced
1 green sweet pepper, seeded and chopped
1 garlic clove, crushed
2 celery stalks, sliced
1 pound ground beef
$1/2 - 1$ teaspoon chili powder
1 tablespoon ground cumin
1 can (28-ounce) chopped tomatoes
1 can (28-ounce) can red kidney beans
$1/4$ pound mushrooms, sliced
salt and pepper
1 large package tortilla chips
2 tomatoes, peeled and cut in chunks
10 green olives, pitted and sliced
1 cup diced mozzarella cheese

Heat the oil in a skillet. Cook half the sliced onion with the green sweet pepper, garlic and celery for 10 minutes. Stir in the beef, chili powder and cumin and cook for 5 minutes, stirring. Turn the mixture into the soaked clay pot. Add the tomatoes, kidney beans and mushrooms with plenty of seasoning. Mix well. Cover the pot and place in the cold oven. Set the oven at 425F. Cook for 50 minutes.

Stir the meat mixture and taste it for seasoning. Sprinkle the reserved onion slices, the tortilla chips, tomatoes, olives and cheese over the top. Cook, uncovered, for a further 10 minutes, or until the topping is bubbling and golden. Serve at once with lots of warm crusty bread.

Serves 4 – 6

ONE-POT PASTA

1 tablespoon oil
1 onion, chopped
1 garlic clove, crushed
1 red sweet pepper, seeded and diced
1 green sweet pepper, seeded and diced
2 carrots, diced
2 celery stalks, diced
1¹/4 cups diced rindless bacon
¹/2 pound ground beef
2¹/2 cups beef stock
1 bay leaf
1 teaspoon dried oregano
salt and pepper
1 can (28-ounce) chopped tomatoes
³/4 pound pasta bows
freshly grated Parmesan cheese, to serve

Heat the oil in a skillet. Add the onion, garlic, sweet peppers, carrots and celery. Cook for 5 minutes, then stir in the bacon and meat, and cook for a further 5 minutes. Turn the mixture into the soaked clay pot. Stir in the stock, herbs, seasoning and tomatoes. Cover the pot and place in the cold oven. Set the oven at 475F. Cook for 50 minutes.

Reduce the oven setting to 400F. Stir the meat mixture well, then stir in the pasta. Cook, covered, for a further 30 minutes, or until the pasta is tender. The mixture should be juicy, neither too wet nor too dry. Taste for seasoning before serving with Parmesan cheese.

Serves 4 – 6

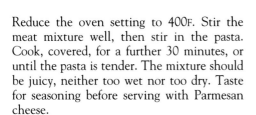

STUFFED VEAL

1 1/2 pounds boned breast or loin of veal
salt and pepper
1 tablespoon lemon juice
1/2 pound sausagemeat
1 egg
1 onion, finely chopped
6 tablespoons fresh bread crumbs
2 tablespoons chopped parsley
1 tablespoon chopped thyme
grated rind of 1/2 lemon
1 cup dry white wine
1 1/2 cups light cream
2 tablespoons chopped dill (optional)
dill sprigs, to garnish (optional)

Trim the veal of excess fat, then season it well all over and sprinkle with lemon juice. Mix together the sausagemeat, egg, onion, bread crumbs, herbs, lemon rind and plenty of seasoning. When all the ingredients are thoroughly combined, spread the stuffing over the meat and roll it up neatly. Tie securely and place in the soaked clay pot. Pour in the wine.

Cover the pot and place in the cold oven. Set the oven at 400F. Cook for 2 1/4 hours, or until the veal is tender. Transfer the meat to a serving platter. Strain the cooking juices into a saucepan and add the cream. Heat gently without boiling, then stir in the dill, if used, and taste for seasoning. Carve the veal, garnish with dill, if used, and serve the sauce separately.

Serves 6

OSSO BUCCO

2 pounds stewing veal
3 tablespoons all-purpose flour
salt and pepper
2 tablespoons oil
1 onion, halved and sliced
2 garlic cloves, crushed
1 bay leaf
1 cup dry white wine
1 cup chicken stock
1 pound tomatoes, peeled and chopped
4 tablespoons chopped parsley
grated rind of 1 lemon

Toss the veal with the flour and plenty of seasoning. Heat the oil in a skillet and brown the meat. Transfer the meat to the soaked clay pot. Add the onion, half the garlic and the bay leaf to the pan and cook for 5 minutes. Stir in the wine, stock and tomatoes. Mix well and pour into the pot. Cover the pot and place in the cold oven. Set the oven at 400F. Cook for 2¹/₂ hours.

Mix together the remaining garlic, parsley and lemon rind. Taste the casserole for seasoning, sprinkle with the parsley mixture and serve.

Serves 4

Note: Authentically, the veal should be on the bone and the pieces of meat arranged so that the bones stand cut-side upright to retain their flavorsome marrow.

ROAST LAMB

4-pound leg of lamb
4 garlic cloves
8 sprigs rosemary
salt and pepper
1 cup red wine
4 tablespoons butter
3 tablespoons all-purpose flour
redcurrant or mint jelly, to serve

Make small deep cuts into the meat. Cut each garlic clove in half or quarters lengthways, then insert the pieces in the slits in the meat. Do the same with the rosemary. Place the joint in the soaked clay pot and season well. Cover the pot and place in the cold oven. Set the oven at 425F. Cook for 1 hour. Heat the wine in a small saucepan until just warm, then pour it over the lamb. Cook, covered, for 30 minutes. Pour 2 cups hot water around the lamb and cook, covered, for a further 40 – 50 minutes.

Meanwhile, beat the butter and flour to a paste. Transfer the meat to a platter, tent with foil and set aside. Strain the cooking liquid into a saucepan and bring to simmering point, gradually add knobs of the butter mixture, whisking all the time. Simmer for 3 minutes, whisking, until thickened. Taste for seasoning. Carve the lamb and serve with seasonal vegetables, the sauce and redcurrant or mint jelly.

Serves 6 – 8

—NOISETTES WITH CALVADOS—

2 tablespoons oil
1 onion, finely chopped
2 eating apples, peeled, cored and sliced
3 cups shelled fresh peas
1 bay leaf
salt and pepper
1 cup cider
4 sprigs mint
8 slices boned and rolled lamb loin
4 tablespoons Calvados or brandy
1 small romaine lettuce, coarsely shredded
mint sprigs, to garnish

Heat half the oil in a skillet. Add the onion and cook for 5 minutes, then mix in the apples, peas, bay leaf and seasoning. Turn the mixture into the soaked clay pot and pour in the cider. Top with the mint sprigs.

Heat the remaining oil in the skillet. Quickly brown the lamb on all sides. Pour the Calvados or brandy over the lamb, set it alight and allow to burn out. Then arrange the lamb on top of the vegetables in the pot. Season well. Cover the pot and place in the cold oven. Set at 425F. Cook for 40 minutes. Add the lettuce and cook for a further 10 minutes. Serve garnished with mint.

Serves 4

IRISH STEW

8 middle neck lamb chops or cutlets
salt and pepper
2 bay leaves
6 sprigs parsley
6 sprigs thyme
4 small sprigs rosemary
2 large onions, thinly sliced
4 – 6 carrots, sliced
4 large potatoes, sliced
lump of butter, melted

Trim any excess fat from the chops, then place four of them in the soaked clay pot. Add plenty of seasoning – this is important. Top with a bay leaf and half the herb sprigs. Add layers of onion, carrot and potato, seasoning each lightly. Then place the remaining lamb in the pot, seasoning well and adding the remaining ingredients as before, ending with a neat layer of potatoes.

Pour in 2^1/$_2$ cups water. Cover the pot and place in the cold oven. Set the oven at 425F. Cook for 2^1/$_2$ hours. Brush the top of the potatoes with butter and cook, uncovered, for a further 20 minutes for extra browning. Serve with buttered cabbage.

Serves 4

Note: Neck of lamb may be used in place of chops or cutlets.

—LAMB WITH CAULIFLOWER—

1 1/2 pounds lean boneless lamb, cubed
3 tablespoons all-purpose flour
salt and pepper
2 tablespoons oil
1 onion, halved and sliced
1 cup lamb or chicken stock
1 cup dry white wine or cider
1/2 teaspoon ground mace
1 cauliflower, broken in small florets
1 tablespoon chopped mint
2 tablespoons chopped fennel
1/2 cup sour cream (optional)
mint and fennel sprigs, to garnish

Toss the lamb with the flour and plenty of seasoning. Heat the oil in a skillet and brown the meat. Add the onion with any remaining flour. Stir for 2 minutes, then pour in the stock and wine. Add half the mint and fennel, and stir well. Transfer to the soaked clay pot. Add the mace. Cover the pot and place in the cold oven. Set the oven at 425F. Cook for 50 minutes.

Add the cauliflower to the pot, stirring the florets into the meat mixture. Cook, covered, for a further 40 minutes, until the lamb is tender and the cauliflower cooked. Taste for seasoning, then lightly mix in the remaining mint and fennel. Serve topped with sour cream (if used) and garnished with mint or fennel, or both. New potatoes and snow peas are excellent accompaniments.

Serves 4

PORK WITH SAUERKRAUT

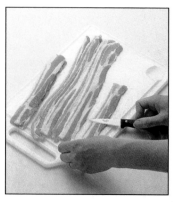

1 garlic clove, crushed
1 teaspoon paprika
salt and pepper
1 pork tenderloin
1/2 pound rindless smoked bacon slices
knob of butter
1 large onion, chopped
1 teaspoon caraway seeds
1 pound sauerkraut
1 cup dry white wine
parsley sprigs, to garnish

Mix together the garlic, paprika and a little seasoning. Rub this mixture all over the pork. Stretch the bacon slices out thinly with the back of a knife. Wrap the slices around the tenderloin, to enclose it completely, tying them neatly in place.

Melt the butter in a small saucepan and cook the onion with the caraway seeds for 5 minutes. Squeeze the liquid from the sauerkraut, then slice it. Place the sauerkraut in the soaked clay pot, then mix in the onion and pour the wine over. Lay the pork on top. Cover the pot and place in the cold oven. Set the oven at 425F. Cook for 50 minutes. Uncover the pot and cook for a further 15 minutes. Untie and slice the pork; serve on the sauerkraut and garnish with parsley.

Serves 4

PORK WITH RED CABBAGE

3 pounds rolled loin of pork
2 teaspoons thyme leaves or $^3/_4$ teaspoon dried thyme
$^1/_4$ teaspoon ground allspice
salt and pepper
2 garlic cloves, crushed
1 tablespoon oil
1 onion, thinly sliced
1 carrot, coarsely grated
1$^1/_2$ pounds red cabbage, shredded
2 cooking apples, peeled, cored and sliced
2 bay leaves
2 tablespoons brown sugar
2 tablespoons wine vinegar
1 cup red wine
2 teaspoons cornstarch

Rub the pork all over with the thyme, allspice, seasoning and garlic. Heat the oil in a large skillet, then roll the pork in it over a high heat to sear the rind. Mix the onion, carrot, cabbage and apples together in the soaked clay pot. Tuck the bay leaves into the vegetables. Sprinkle with seasoning, add the sugar, vinegar and wine. Place the pork, with the oil from searing, on top of the cabbage mixture. Cover the pot and place in the cold oven. Set the oven at 425F. Cook for 1$^1/_2$ hours.

Mix the cornstarch with a little water, then add a little of the cooking liquor before stirring the mixture into the vegetables and their juices around the pork. Cook, covered, for 15 minutes, then uncover the pot and cook for a final 15 minutes. Transfer the meat to a serving platter and serve cut in thick slices. Turn the cabbage into a serving dish. Creamy mashed potatoes are an excellent accompaniment.

Serves 6

—PORK HOTPOT WITH SALSA—

1 pound lean boneless pork, cubed
3 tablespoons all-purpose flour
salt and pepper
4 tablespoons olive oil
4 sprigs sage
2 onions, finely chopped
1 cup cider
4 large potatoes, diced
4 cups peeled and chopped tomatoes
1 green chili, seeded and chopped
1 garlic clove, crushed
1 tablespoon superfine sugar
1 tablespoon lime or lemon juice
1 tablespoon sesame seeds
4 tablespoons chopped parsley
$1/2$ cup light cream

Toss the pork with the flour and plenty of seasoning. Heat half the oil in a skillet and brown the pork, then transfer to the soaked clay pot. Fry the sage and half the chopped onion in the oil remaining in the pan, then stir in any leftover flour and the cider. Pour this sauce over the pork. Mix in the potatoes. Cover the pot and place in the cold oven. Set the oven at 425F. Cook for $1^1/2$ hours.

Mix the remaining onion and oil with the tomato, chili, garlic, superfine sugar, lime or lemon juice and seasoning. Heat the sesame seeds in a small saucepan until they are lightly browned, shaking often. Tip the sesame seeds into the tomato salsa and stir well. Set aside for at least 1 hour. Taste the pork for seasoning and add the parsley. Stir in the cream and serve at once, with the salsa to top individual portions.

Serves 4

—PORK CHOPS WITH PUMPKIN—

1 tablespoon oil
1 large onion, chopped
3 cups cubed pumpkin flesh
1 teaspoon ground cinnamon
grated nutmeg
salt and pepper
4 pork chops
4 sprigs rosemary
grated rind and juice of 1 orange
halved orange slices, to garnish

Heat the oil in a large skillet. Add the onion and cook for 2 minutes, stir in the pumpkin, then turn the mixture into the soaked clay pot. Sprinkle with cinnamon, a little grated nutmeg and seasoning. Lay the pork chops on top and tuck the rosemary in between them. Season the chops, then pour the orange rind and juice over.

Cover the pot and place in the cold oven. Set the oven at 450F. Cook for 1 hour. Baste the chops with the cooking juices and cook, uncovered, for a further 5 – 10 minutes. Garnish with orange slices and the rosemary sprigs used in cooking. Baked potatoes topped with sour cream or soft cheese taste terrific with the slightly spicy pork and pumpkin.

Serves 4

— SPICY PORK WITH BANANA —

1½ pounds lean boneless pork, diced
1 tablespoon ground coriander
1 teaspoon paprika
¼ teaspoon ground cloves
1 teaspoon ground mace
salt and pepper
2 garlic cloves, crushed
1 teaspoon sesame oil
2 tablespoons sunflower oil
grated rind and juice of 1 lime
1 cup coconut milk
2 plantains or unripe bananas, halved lengthways and
    sliced
2 tablespoons chopped cilantro
1 lime, cut in wedges

Place the pork in a bowl. Add the coriander, paprika, cloves, mace, seasoning, garlic, both oils and the lime rind and juice. Mix well, cover and leave to marinate for 24 hours. Tip the mixture into the soaked clay pot. Pour in the coconut milk and stir well. Cover the pot and place in the cold oven. Set the oven at 450F. Cook for 45 minutes. Then add the plantains, if used, and mix lightly.

Cook, covered, for a further 20 minutes. If using bananas, which require less cooking than plantains, stir them in at this stage. Finally, cook, uncovered for 10 minutes. Sprinkle with the chopped cilantro and serve at once, with lime wedges for their juice.

Serves 4

— SWEET 'N' SPICY SPARERIBS —

4 pounds meaty spareribs
8 carrots
1 onion, finely chopped
2 tablespoons clear honey
juice of 1 lemon
1 tablespoon good-quality curry powder
salt and pepper

Place the spareribs in the soaked clay pot. Cut the carrots in half, then quarter the pieces lengthways. Add the carrots and sprinkle the chopped onion over the top. Mix together the honey, lemon juice, curry powder and plenty of seasoning, then trickle the mixture evenly over the spareribs. Cover the pot and place in the cold oven. Set the oven at 475F. Cook for 1 hour.

Transfer the carrots to a serving dish and keep hot. Rearrange the spareribs and baste them with the juices, then cook, uncovered, rearranging the ribs once more, for a further 20 minutes, or until well browned. Serve piping hot.

Serves 4

GLAZED MEATBALLS

1 pound ground pork
1 cup fresh bread crumbs
3/4 cup chopped mushrooms
4 tablespoons crunchy peanut butter
2 tablespoons chopped parsley
1 teaspoon dried marjoram
1 garlic clove, crushed
salt and pepper
1 egg, beaten
1 pound pearl onions
2 tablespoons oil
1 cup beer
1 bay leaf
1 tablespoon Worcestershire sauce
2 tablespoons tomato ketchup
1 tablespoon brown sugar

Place the pork, bread crumbs, mushrooms, peanut butter, parsley, marjoram, garlic and seasoning in a bowl. Mix well, then add the egg and mix it in to bind the ingredients. Wet your hands and shape the mixture into small balls, slightly larger than the pearl onions. Heat the oil in a skillet, quickly brown the meatballs and transfer to the soaked clay pot. Brown the onions and add to the pot. Pour the beer into the pan, stir well, then pour it into the pot.

Add the bay leaf, Worcestershire sauce and ketchup to the meatball mixture. Sprinkle with a little seasoning and the sugar. Cover the pot and place in the cold oven. Set the oven at 425F. Cook for 1 hour, stirring once. Serve garnished with the bay leaf or other fresh herbs if liked. Rice or couscous and a crisp salad are ideal with the meatballs.

Serves 4

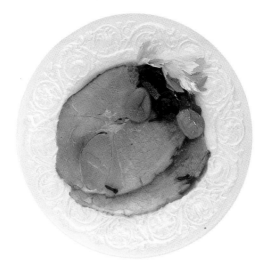

GLAZED HAM

3-pound boned and rolled picnic ham
1 onion, quartered
1 carrot, sliced
4 tablespoons orange marmalade
1 tablespoon dry mustard
2 tablespoons brown sugar
1 tablespoon sherry
1 tablespoon cloves
12 ready-to-eat prunes
12 ready-to-eat dried apricots
$^1/_2$ cup red wine

Place the ham in a large saucepan with the onion and carrot. Cover with cold water, bring to a boil and skim any scum from the surface. Cover and simmer for 1 hour. Drain, remove the rind and score the fat in diamond shapes. Melt the marmalade in a small saucepan, then mix with the mustard, sugar and sherry. Coat the ham with this mixture and stud with cloves.

Place the ham in the soaked clay pot. Add the prunes and apricots and pour the wine over the fruit. Cover the pot and place in the cold oven. Set the oven at 425F. Cook for 1 hour. Serve the glazed prunes and apricots with the ham.

Serves 6 – 8

HAM WITH CUCUMBER

1 pound lean uncooked ham, cut in strips
1 onion, halved and thinly sliced
1 green sweet pepper, seeded, quartered lengthways
    and thinly sliced
1 pound gourmet cucumber, peeled and cut into
    fingers
salt and pepper
2 tablespoons olive oil
4 tablespoons dry sherry
4 tablespoons shelled pistachio nuts
2 tablespoons capers
4 tablespoons Greek-style yoghurt
2 tablespoons chopped dill
dill sprigs, to garnish (optional)

Place the ham in the soaked clay pot. Add the onion, green sweet pepper and cucumber. Sprinkle in seasoning, add the oil and sherry and toss the ingredients together well. Cover the pot and place in the cold oven. Set the oven at 425F. Cook for 40 minutes.

Stir the ham mixture well. Sprinkle the pistachio nuts and capers over the ham mixture. Cook, covered, for a further 30 minutes, until the vegetables are tender. Top with the yoghurt, add the chopped dill and stir lightly. Serve garnished with dill sprigs, if liked.

Serves 4

POTATOES ANNA

4 – 5 pounds potatoes, finely sliced
1/2 cup melted butter
salt and pepper

The exact quantity of potatoes will depend on the size of your clay pot. Brush the soaked pot with butter, then layer the potatoes, seasoning each layer well and adding a little butter here and there. Trickle the remaining butter over the top and press down well with the back of a spoon.

Cover the pot and place in the cold oven. Set the oven at 425F. Cook for 1 1/2 hours. Uncover the pot and cook for a further 15 minutes. To serve, slide a spatula between the potatoes and the pot. Invert the pot on a large platter, then lift it off to reveal the golden potato cake. Cut into wedges to serve.

Serves 8 – 10

—CABBAGE-POTATO FAVORITE—

1 1/2 pounds cabbage, shredded
2 onions, thinly sliced
4 large potatoes, thinly sliced
1/2 pound rindless bacon slices, diced (optional)
2 bay leaves
salt and pepper
1 cup milk
lump of butter, melted

Layer the cabbage, onions, potatoes and bacon (if used) in the soaked clay pot, ending with a layer of potato on top. Add the bay leaves somewhere around the middle of the pot and season the layers well, especially if the bacon is not used. Pour the milk over. Cover the pot and place in the cold oven. Set the oven at 425F. Cook for 1 hour.

Brush the potatoes with butter and cook, uncovered, for a further 15 minutes or until golden brown.

Serves 4

Note: Thinly sliced smoked sausage is delicious layered with the potatoes.

—POTATOES WITH PINE NUTS—

2 pounds small new potatoes, scrubbed
2 small red onions, thinly sliced
2 tablespoons currants
3 tablespoons pine nuts
2 tablespoons olive oil
2 garlic cloves, crushed
12 black olives, pitted and sliced
1 bay leaf
salt and pepper
1/2 cup red vermouth
about 2 tablespoons shredded basil
basil sprigs, to garnish

Place the potatoes in the soaked clay pot. Mix in the onions, currants, pine nuts and olive oil. Add the garlic, olives and bay leaf with a generous sprinkling of seasoning. Pour in the vermouth. Cover the pot and place in the cold oven. Set the oven at 450F. Cook for 1 hour, or until the potatoes are tender.

Leave the potatoes to stand in the pot, without removing the lid, for 10 minutes. Then mix in the shredded basil and garnish with the whole sprigs.

Serves 4 – 6

-CUMIN POTATOES WITH PEAS-

2 pounds small new potatoes, scrubbed
1 large onion, chopped
2 tablespoons cumin seeds
2 tablespoons oil or melted ghee
juice of 1 lemon
salt and pepper
1/2 pound frozen peas
2 tablespoons chopped mint

Place the potatoes in the soaked clay pot. Add the onion, cumin seeds, oil or ghee and lemon juice. Sprinkle in plenty of seasoning. Cover the pot and place in the cold oven. Set the oven at 475F. Cook for 40 minutes.

Add the peas to the pot, mixing them with the potatoes. Cook, covered, for a further 15 minutes, or until the potatoes are tender and the peas are lightly cooked. Stand for 10 minutes, without removing the lid, then mix in the mint and serve.

Serves 4 – 6

GLAZED CARROTS

1¹/2 pounds carrots, cut into fingers
1 tablespoon sugar
salt and pepper
juice of 1 orange
4 tablespoons melted butter
1 tablespoon chopped tarragon
2 tablespoons snipped chives
tarragon sprigs, to garnish (optional)

Place the carrots in the soaked clay pot. Sprinkle the sugar and seasoning over the carrots, then pour in the orange juice. Add the melted butter. Cover the pot and place in the cold oven. Set the oven at 425F. Cook for 25 minutes.

Stir the carrots and cook, uncovered, for a further 10 minutes. Sprinkle with the herbs and garnish with tarragon sprigs, if liked. Serve at once.

Serves 4

BROCCOLI CREAM

1 pound young broccoli florets
3 tablespoons snipped chives
1 cup grated cheese
3 eggs
salt and pepper
1¹/₂ cups light cream
4 tablespoons fresh bread crumbs
2 tablespoons melted butter
chives, to garnish (optional)

Blanch the broccoli in boiling water for 2 minutes, then drain well. Place in the soaked clay pot. Sprinkle the chives and two-thirds of the cheese over the broccoli. Beat the eggs with plenty of seasoning. Add the cream, then pour the mixture over the broccoli. Cover the pot and place in the cold oven. Set the oven at 425F. Cook for 30 minutes, or until the custard is set.

Mix the remaining cheese with the bread crumbs. Sprinkle this over the top of the broccoli mixture, then trickle the butter over. Cook, uncovered, for a further 10 – 15 minutes, or until crisp and golden brown. Serve at once, garnished with chives, if liked.

Serves 4

CLASSIC RATATOUILLE

2 eggplants, cubed
salt and pepper
1/2 cup olive oil
1 green sweet pepper, seeded, halved and sliced
1 large onion, halved and sliced
1 garlic clove, crushed
1 teaspoon dried marjoram
1/2 pound zucchini, thickly sliced
2 pounds tomatoes, peeled and quartered
1 bay leaf
4 tablespoons chopped parsley

Sprinkle the eggplant cubes with salt and leave to stand for 20 minutes. Rinse and drain well. Heat some of the oil in a large skillet. Add the sweet pepper, onion, garlic and marjoram and cook for 3 minutes. Use a slotted spoon to transfer the mixture to the soaked clay pot. Add some eggplant cubes to the oil left in the pan and brown them quickly on all sides. Continue browning the eggplant, adding more oil as necessary. Tip the eggplant into the pot.

Add the zucchini, tomatoes and bay leaf to the pot. Mix well and add a good sprinkling of seasoning. Cover the pot and place in the cold oven. Set the oven at 425F. Cook for 1 hour. Leave to stand, out of the oven, without removing the lid, for 20 minutes before serving. Taste for seasoning, then mix in the parsley and serve.

Serves 6

—RICH VEGETABLE RAGOUT—

lump of butter
4 leeks, sliced
2 celery stalks, sliced
2 large potatoes, cut in large dice
2 carrots, halved and sliced
2 parsnips, halved and sliced
$1/2$ cauliflower, broken into florets
1 can (14-ounce) chick peas, drained
2 tablespoons tomato paste
1 cup dry cider
1 tablespoon sugar
salt and pepper
1 bay leaf
1 cup grated cheese
4 tablespoons fresh bread crumbs
2 tablespoons sesame seeds

Melt the butter in a large saucepan. Add the leeks and celery, and cook for 5 minutes, until the leeks are softened and reduced in volume. Turn the leek mixture into the soaked clay pot. Add all the remaining vegetables and the chick peas. Mix the ingredients together well. Stir the tomato paste, cider and sugar together, then add a generous sprinkling of seasoning and pour the mixture over the vegetables. Tuck the bay leaf into the ingredients.

Cover the pot and place in the cold oven. Set the oven at 425F. Cook for 1 hour. Stir well and taste for seasoning. Mix together the cheese, bread crumbs and sesame seeds. Sprinkle this topping over the ragout and cook, uncovered, for a further 15 minutes, or until the topping is golden and the vegetables are tender.

Serves 4 – 6

PUMPKIN WITH CHORIZO

1 large onion, finely chopped
1 1/2 pounds pumpkin flesh, cubed
1/2 pound small button mushrooms
3/4 pound chorizo, sliced
salt and pepper
2 bay leaves
4 sprigs thyme
2 avocados
juice of 1 lime
1 teaspoon sugar
1 cup sour cream (optional)
lime slices and thyme sprigs, to garnish

Place the onion, pumpkin, mushrooms and chorizo in the soaked clay pot. Mix in seasoning, then add the bay leaf and thyme. Sprinkle 1/2 cup water over the pumpkin mixture. Cover the pot and place in the cold oven. Set the oven at 425F. Cook for 1 hour, or until the pumpkin is tender.

Just before the pumpkin is cooked, halve the avocados and remove the pits. Peel and dice the flesh, then mix it with the lime juice and sugar. Serve the pumpkin mixture topped with the sour cream (if used) and diced avocado mixture.

Serves 4 – 6

—BAKED BUTTERNUT SQUASH—

2 small butternut squash
4 tablespoons melted butter
1 tablespoon lemon juice
salt and pepper
4 tablespoons walnut oil
4 tablespoons dry sherry
4 tablespoons chopped parsley
2 tablespoons snipped chives
2 tablespoons chopped walnuts
2 tablespoons fresh bread crumbs
2 tablespoons grated Parmesan cheese
parsley sprigs, to garnish

Cut the squash in half lengthways. Scoop any small amount of fiber from the central hole, then place the squash halves in the soaked clay pot. Trickle the butter and lemon juice over the cut surface of each half, then season lightly. Cover the pot and place in the cold oven. Set the oven at 425F. Cook for 45 minutes.

Mix the walnut oil and sherry with the parsley and chives. Spoon this over the squash halves. Sprinkle with the walnuts, bread crumbs and Parmesan and cook, un-covered, for a further 15 minutes, or until the topping is crisp and golden and the squash is tender. Serve garnished with parsley.

Serves 4

STUFFED SQUASH

2 tablespoons oil
1 large onion, chopped
1/2 teaspoon dried oregano
salt and pepper
1/3 cup rice
1/2 cup chicken or vegetable stock
1 small summer squash, peeled
1 can (14-ounce) chopped tomatoes
2 tablespoons currants
4 tablespoons pine nuts
1 garlic clove, crushed
4 tablespoons grated Parmesan cheese
4 tablespoons chopped parsley

Heat the oil in a small saucepan, add the onion and cook for 2 minutes. Stir in the oregano, seasoning, rice and stock. Bring just to a boil, reduce the heat and cover the pan. Simmer for 20 minutes. Meanwhile, halve the squash and discard the seeds. Place the squash halves side by side in the soaked clay pot.

Mix the tomatoes, currants, pine nuts, garlic, Parmesan cheese and most of the parsley with the rice mixture, then spoon this into the hollows in the squash halves. Cover the pot and place in the cold oven. Set the oven at 450F. Cook for 50 – 60 minutes, or until the squash is tender. Sprinkle with the remaining parsley.

Serves 4 – 6

STUFFED PEPPERS

4 green sweet peppers
$^1/_2$ pound pork sausagemeat
$^1/_2$ pound ground beef
1 tablespoon dried basil
3 tablespoons chopped sage or 1 tablespoon
    dried sage
1 cup fresh bread crumbs
1 onion, chopped
1 egg
salt and pepper
sage sprigs and tomato wedges, to garnish

Slice the tops off the sweet peppers and set aside, then scoop out all the seeds and pith from inside. Rinse and drain upside down. Mix together the sausagemeat, beef, basil, sage, bread crumbs, onion and egg. Add plenty of seasoning and make sure all the ingredients are thoroughly combined. Divide the mixture into quarters and pack one portion into each of the sweet peppers. Replace the tops on the sweet peppers and stand them in the soaked clay pot.

Cover the pot and place in the cold oven. Set the oven at 475F. Cook for 50 minutes, or until the sweet peppers are thoroughly tender and the meat filling is cooked through. Serve piping hot, with rice or pasta tossed with Parmesan cheese. Garnish with sage and tomato.

Serves 4

NOODLE BAKE

¹/₂ pound egg noodles, cooked
¹/₂ pound cooked ham, shredded
¹/₂ pound green beans, lightly cooked
¹/₂ pound mushrooms, sliced
1 can (14-ounce) corn
4 scallions, chopped
2 tablespoons chopped parsley
salt and pepper
1 cup grated cheese
1 egg
1 cup light cream

The noodles should be cooked until only just tender – if they are too soft, they will lose their texture by the time the bake is ready. Place half the noodles in a layer in the bottom of the soaked clay pot. Mix the ham with all the vegetables, parsley and seasoning. Then spread the mixture in an even layer over the noodles. Top with half the cheese, then cover with the remaining noodles.

Press the noodles down evenly and sprinkle the remaining cheese over. Beat the egg with the cream and pour it over the top. Cover the pot and place in the cold oven. Set the oven at 475F. Cook for 30 minutes. Uncover the pot and cook for 15 minutes, or until the top of the noodles is crisp and golden. Serve at once, with a green salad.

Serves 4

SULTAN'S PILAF

lump of butter
1 pound lean boneless lamb, diced
2 onions, sliced
1 garlic clove
1 cinnamon stick
4 cloves
1 bay leaf
pared rind of 1 lemon
salt and pepper
2¹/₂ cups chicken stock
1 cup dry white wine
¹/₂ pound long-grain rice
2 tablespoons chopped dried dates
¹/₂ pound frozen peas
4 hard-cooked eggs, quartered
1 lemon, cut in wedges

Melt the butter in a large skillet. Brown the lamb all over, then use a slotted spoon to transfer the meat to the soaked clay pot. Add the onions to the fat in the pan and cook for 2 minutes, then transfer two-thirds to the pot and continue cooking the remainder until golden-brown. Drain and set aside. Add a little of the stock to the skillet, stir well, then pour it into the pot. Add the remaining stock, garlic, spices, bay leaf and lemon rind. Season well.

Cover the pot and place in the cold oven. Set the oven at 425F. Cook for 1 hour, or until the meat is extremely tender. Add the wine, rice and dates, and cook, covered, for a further 15 minutes. Stir in the peas, cook, covered, for a final 20 minutes, then leave to stand, without removing the lid, for 15 minutes. Serve the pilaf garnished with the eggs, lemon wedges and reserved onions.

Serves 4 – 6

TUNA BAKE

$^{1}/_{2}$ pound long-grain rice
1 onion, chopped
1 green sweet pepper, seeded and diced
$2^{1}/_{2}$ cups vegetable or chicken stock
salt and pepper
1 can (14-ounce) corn
1 can (8-ounce) tuna, drained and flaked
1 cup light cream or Greek-style
yoghurt
1 cup grated cheese
parsley sprigs, to garnish

Mix the rice, onion and green sweet pepper in the soaked clay pot. Pour in the stock and add seasoning to taste. Cover the pot and place in the cold oven. Set the oven at 425F. Cook for 40 minutes, or until the rice is almost tender and most of the stock is absorbed.

Fork the corn, tuna, cream or yoghurt and two-thirds of the cheese into the rice. Sprinkle the remaining cheese over the top and cook, uncovered, for a further 10 minutes, or until lightly browned. Garnish with parsley and serve with a crisp green salad.

Serves 4

STUFFED VINE LEAVES

^{1}/$_2$ pound package vine leaves in brine, drained
^{3}/$_4$ cup long-grain rice
1 bay leaf
1 lemon
4 tablespoons olive oil
1 onion, chopped
2 garlic cloves, crushed
2 tablespoons currants
2 tablespoons pine nuts
2 teaspoons oregano
salt and pepper
1^1/$_2$ cups dry white wine

Blanch the vine leaves in boiling water for 3 minutes, drain them and rinse under cold water, then leave to drain. Place the rice in a saucepan with the bay leaf. Pare the lemon rind, add it to the rice with plenty of cold water. Bring to a boil and cook for 10 minutes, then drain. Set aside the bay leaf and lemon, cut into wedges. Heat half the oil in a skillet. Add the onion, garlic, currants and pine nuts, and cook for 5 minutes. Stir in plenty of seasoning and the rice.

Place a small spoonful of rice in the middle of a vine leaf (about a heaped teaspoonful). Fold the sides over, then roll it up and place in the soaked clay pot. Stuff all the leaves. Pour in the wine and trickle the oil over. Add the bay leaf and lemon rind. Cover the pot and place in the cold oven. Set the oven at 425F. Cook for 1 hour, or until the leaves are tender and most of the liquid is absorbed. Serve hot or cold.

Makes about 35

PORK CHILI

1 pound lean boneless pork, diced
2 tablespoons all-purpose flour
2 teaspoons ground cumin
1 teaspoon oregano
salt and pepper
2 tablespoons oil
2 garlic cloves, crushed
2 onions, halved and sliced
2 – 4 canned jalapeño chilies, chopped
2 cans (14-ounce) red kidney beans, drained
1 cup vegetable stock
2 avocados
2 tablespoons chopped cilantro
1 tablespoon chopped mint
1 lime, cut in wedges

Mix the pork with the flour, cumin, oregano and plenty of seasoning. Heat the oil in a skillet and quickly brown the meat. Add the garlic and onions and cook for 2 minutes, then turn the mixture into the soaked clay pot. Add the chilies (see note), kidney beans and stock. Cover the pot and place in the cold oven. Set the oven at 450F. Cook for 1¼ hours, or until the meat is very tender.

When the chili is cooked, halve, pit and peel the avocados, then slice them. Top each portion of chili with cilantro, mint and avocado. Serve lime wedges for their juice.

Serves 4

Note: Make the chili as hot as you like by adding more jalapeño chilies. Canned jalapeños are quite mild and a whole, small, can will not make the dish too fiery. Fresh chilies are very hot.

BUTTER BEAN HOTPOT

^{1}/2 pound dried butter beans, soaked overnight
1 bay leaf
1 sprig thyme
1 tablespoon chopped sage
^{1}/4 tsp ground mace
2 carrots, thickly sliced
2 celery stalks, sliced
2 onions, halved and thinly sliced
2^{1}/2 cups unsalted chicken or vegetable stock
salt and pepper
^{1}/4 pound salami, shredded (optional)
1 cup fresh bread crumbs
^{1}/2 cup grated cheese

Drain the beans, place in a saucepan with plenty of cold water and bring to a boil. Boil rapidly for 10 minutes, then drain and place in the soaked clay pot. Add the herbs, mace, carrots, celery and onions, in that order without mixing the ingredients. Pour in the stock. Cover the pot and place in the cold oven. Set the oven at 425F. Cook for 1 – 1 ^{1}/4 hours, or until the beans are tender.

Add seasoning to taste and stir the beans with the vegetables. Sprinkle the salami over (if used), then mix the bread crumbs and cheese together and sprinkle the mixture over the top. Cook, uncovered, for a further 15 minutes, to brown the topping before serving.

Serves 4 – 6

Note: If salt or seasoned stock is used, the beans will become tough and will not soften no matter how long they are cooked.

BUCKWHEAT PILAF

lump of butter
1 onion, chopped
1 garlic clove, crushed
1/4 pound ready-to-eat dried apricots, roughly
    chopped
2 tablespoons sultanas
1/2 pound roasted buckwheat
2 1/2 cups chicken stock
salt and pepper
1/2 pound smoked pork, diced
3/4 cup diced cooked chicken
3/4 cup diced, lean cooked ham
2 tablespoons chopped parsley
4 – 6 tablespoons plain yoghurt
parsley sprigs, to garnish

Melt the butter in a small saucepan. Add the onion and garlic, cook for 2 minutes, then stir in the apricots and sultanas. Cook for another 2 minutes. Place the buckwheat in the soaked clay pot, add the onion mixture and pour in the stock. Add seasoning and stir well.

Cover the pot and place in the cold oven. Set the oven at 425F. Cook for 20 minutes. Sprinkle with the pork, chicken and ham and cook, covered, for a further 10 minutes. Leave to stand, without removing the lid, for 10 minutes, then fork the meat and parsley into the buckwheat and serve topped with the yoghurt, if liked. Garnish with parsley.

Serves 4

COUSCOUS TURNABOUT

1 onion, chopped
1 red sweet pepper, seeded and chopped
2 tablespoons olive oil
$^{1}/_{2}$ pound ground beef
$^{1}/_{2}$ cup diced rindless bacon slices
2 tablespoons chopped salted peanuts
1 pound zucchini, cut in chunks
1 can (14-ounce) chopped tomatoes
salt and pepper
$^{1}/_{2}$ pound couscous
3 tablespoons grated Parmesan cheese
3 tablespoons dry white bread crumbs

Mix the onion, red sweet pepper and olive oil in the soaked clay pot. Add the beef, bacon and peanuts. Mix well, breaking up the meat. Place the pot, uncovered, in the cold oven. Set the oven at 450F. Cook for 20 minutes. Stir in the zucchini, tomatoes and seasoning and cook, covered, for a further 20 minutes.

Meanwhile, put the couscous in a bowl and pour in enough boiling water to cover it by 1 inch. Leave to stand for 20 minutes. Spread the couscous over the top of the beef and zucchini mixture in an even layer. Mix the Parmesan and bread crumbs together and sprinkle over the top. Cook, uncovered, for 10 minutes to brown the top, before serving.

Serves 4 – 6

——RED LENTIL FLORENTINE——

1 onion, chopped
1 bay leaf
$^1/_2$ pound red lentils
$2^1/_2$ cups chicken or vegetable stock
salt and pepper
1 pound spinach, trimmed and washed
large lump of butter
grated nutmeg
1 tablespoon all-purpose flour
4 tablespoons grated Parmesan cheese
1 cup light cream
6 hard-cooked eggs, halved

Mix the onion, bay leaf and lentils in the soaked clay pot. Add the stock and seasoning. Cover the pot and place in the cold oven. Set the oven at 450F. Cook for 35 minutes, or until most of the stock is absorbed and the lentils are just cooked. Meanwhile, pack the wet spinach into a large saucepan. Cover and cook for 4 – 5 minutes, until the leaves are wilted, shaking the pan often.

Drain and shred the spinach, then toss it with a large knob of butter, seasoning and a little grated nutmeg. Mix the flour, Parmesan and a little seasoning in a bowl, then gradually add the cream, whisking until smooth. Top the lentils in the pot with the spinach and eggs. Pour over the cream and cook, uncovered, for 10 minutes until golden-brown. Serve at once.

Serves 4

BAKED APPLES

4 large cooking apples, cored
4 tablespoons brown sugar
1 teaspoon ground cinnamon
4 tablespoons mixed dried fruit
grated rind and juice of 1 orange
2 tablespoons melted butter
whipped cream or custard, to serve

Score the skin all around the apples, check that all the core is removed from the middle of the fruit and that they stand neatly. Place a piece of non-stick baking parchment in the bottom of the soaked clay pot, then stand the apples on it. Mix together the sugar, cinnamon, dried fruit and orange rind and juice. Stuff this mixture into the core holes in the apples, pressing it down well. Spoon the orange juice over, then trickle the melted butter over.

Cover the pot and place in the cold oven. Set the oven at 475F. Cook for 40 – 50 minutes, or until the apples are tender but not collapsed. The time varies according to the size and particular type of apple, so check at 40 and 45 minutes. Serve with whipped cream or custard.

Serves 4

STEWED APPLE SPECIAL

1 pound cooking apples, peeled, cored and sliced
$^1/_4$ cup superfine sugar
$^1/_2$ pound ready-to-eat dried apricots, roughly
    chopped
2 tablespoons slivered almonds
cream or custard, to serve

Layer the apples, sugar and apricots in the soaked clay pot. Cover the pot and place in the cold oven. Set the oven at 425F. Cook for 40 minutes, or until the apples are soft.

Sprinkle the almonds over the top and cook for a further 5 – 10 minutes. Serve with cream or custard.

Serves 4

Note: Without the apricots, the plain stewed apples may be beaten until smooth to make apple sauce. Chopped walnuts or crumbled chocolate wheatmeal biscuits may be sprinkled over the apples instead of the slivered almonds.

IMPRESSIVE BANANAS

4 large firm bananas
juice of 1 lemon
$^1/_4$ cup brown sugar
$^1/_4$ cup butter
4 tablespoons brandy
4 tablespoons chopped mixed candied fruit (see note)
whipped cream or ice cream, to serve

Halve the bananas lengthways, place in the soaked clay pot and sprinkle with the lemon juice. Top with the sugar and dot with the butter. Cover the pot and place in the cold oven. Set the oven at 425F. Cook for 30 – 35 minutes, or until the sugar has melted and the bananas are hot and juicy.

Pour the brandy over and set it alight. When the flames have subsided, transfer the bananas to serving plates and top with candied fruit. Add whipped cream or ice cream and serve at once.

Serves 4

Note: Angelica, cherries, pineapple, candied peel and ginger are all suitable. Look out for cartons of mixed candied fruit with ginger.

FESTIVE WINTER FRUIT

1 pound mixed dried fruit
1 bottle red wine
2 cardamoms
1 cinnamon stick
pared rind and juice of 1 orange
4 tablespoons brandy
2 – 4 tablespoons clear honey

Place the fruit in a bowl. Pour in the wine and, if necessary, add just enough water to cover the fruit. Cover and leave overnight.

Turn the fruit into the soaked clay pot, with all the soaking liquid. Add the cardamoms and cinnamon, then stir in the orange juice. Shred half the rind finely and add it to the fruit. Cover the pot and place in the cold oven. Set the oven at 375F. Cook for 1 hour, or until the fruit and rind is tender. Stir in the brandy and honey to taste before serving. The compote is also good cold.

Serves 8

— RHUBARB & FIG COMPOTE —

2 pounds tender rhubarb, trimmed
$^1/_2$ cup superfine sugar
3 tablespoons chopped crystallized ginger
1 can (14-ounce) green figs in syrup
6 small sprigs mint

Cut the rhubarb into 2-inch lengths, then place them in the soaked clay pot with the sugar and ginger. Drain the canned figs and pour the syrup over the rhubarb.

Cover the pot and place in the cold oven. Set the oven at 425F. Cook for 40 minutes, or until the rhubarb is tender but not mushy. The cooking time will vary – older, thick rhubarb takes longer than tender young fruit.

Gently mix the figs and 2 of the mint sprigs with the rhubarb and cook, covered, for 5 minutes to heat the figs and give the compote a refreshing mint taste. Decorate individual portions with a mint sprig when serving.

Serves 4

APPLE PIE PUFF

2 pounds cooking apples, peeled, cored and sliced
$1/2$ cup superfine sugar
4 tablespoons raisins
4 tablespoons chopped candied citron peel
grated rind and juice of 1 orange
6 cloves
$1/2$ pound package puff pastry, thawed if frozen
milk and superfine sugar, to glaze

Layer the apples, sugar, raisins and candied citron peel in the soaked clay pot. Sprinkle the orange rind and juice between the layers, adding the cloves somewhere about the middle of the filling. Roll out the dough 2 inches larger than the pot. Trim 1 inch off the edge of the dough, then dampen the rim of the pot and press the dough trimmings on it. Dampen the dough rim. Cover with the rolled-out dough and press the edges together.

Flute the dough edge. Make a small hole in the middle, then glaze with milk and sprinkle with superfine sugar. Place in the cold oven. Set the oven at 425F and cook for 30 minutes. Reduce the temperature to 325F and cook for a further 10 minutes until the apples are tender.
Note: Depending on the size of the pot, the dough may have to be fixed below the rim to lay on top of the fruit. Alternatively, increase the quantity of apples.

Serves 8

PEACH BERRY COBBLER

1 pound blackberries
2/3 cup superfine sugar, plus extra for sprinkling
5 fresh peaches
1 cinnamon stick
1 1/2 cups self-rising flour
3 tablespoons butter or margarine
about 1/2 cup milk
a little lemon juice

Place the blackberries and 1/2 cup of the sugar in the soaked clay pot. Peel, pit and slice 4 of the peaches, then add them to the pot with the cinnamon stick. Mix the fruit together. Cover the pot and place in the cold oven. Set the oven at 425F. Cook for 40 minutes, or until the blackberries are cooked.

Place the flour in a bowl and rub in the shortening. Mix in the remaining sugar and enough milk to make a soft dough. Roll out thickly and cut out 1 1/2-inch round biscuits. Overlap these on top of the fruit. Brush with milk and sprinkle with sugar, then cook, uncovered, for a further 15 – 20 minutes, or until the biscuits are cooked. Pit and slice the remaining peach, toss with lemon juice, then use to decorate the cooked cobbler.

Serves 6

—PINEAPPLE & PEAR CRUNCH—

8 firm pears, peeled, cored and sliced
1 can (8-ounce) pineapple chunks in syrup
$^2/_3$ cup all-purpose flour
$^1/_4$ cup butter
1 cup crushed coconut cookies
Greek-style yoghurt, to serve

Place the pears in the soaked clay pot, then add the pineapple and the syrup from the can.

Place the flour in a bowl. Rub in the butter, then stir in the crushed cookies. Sprinkle this mixture over the fruit in the pot. Cover the pot and place in the cold oven. Set the oven at 425F. Cook for 30 minutes. Uncover the pot and cook for a further 10 minutes, or until crisp on top. The pears should be tender. Serve with Greek-style yoghurt.

Serves 4 – 6

—CHOCOLATE NUT DELIGHT—

oil for greasing
1 cup self-rising flour
4 tablespoons cocoa powder
$^{1}/_{2}$ cup superfine sugar
$^{1}/_{2}$ cup whipped butter or margarine
2 teaspoons natural vanilla extract
2 cups finely chopped walnuts
2 eggs
3 tablespoons clear honey or corn syrup
$^{1}/_{2}$ pound strawberries
3 tablespoons confectioners' sugar
1 tablespoon lemon juice
1 teaspoon ground cinnamon
fresh fruit, to serve (optional)

Cut a piece of non-stick baking parchment to fit the base of the soaked 3 – 5-pound clay pot, then place it in position. Grease the side of the pot. Mix the flour, cocoa powder and superfine sugar in a bowl. Add the shortening, vanilla, half the walnuts and the eggs. Beat the mixture well, preferably using an electric mixer, until soft, slightly paler in color and light. Turn the mixture into the pot and spread it evenly. Sprinkle the rest of the nuts over the top.

Cover the pot and place in the cold oven. Set the oven at 400F. Cook for 50 minutes. The chocolate sponge should feel firm and springy. Trickle the honey or syrup over and cook, covered, for 5 minutes. Meanwhile, purée the strawberries with the confectioners' sugar, lemon juice and cinnamon. Cut the pudding into squares to serve. Top with whipped cream and serve with fresh fruit if you like, for example, raspberries, strawberries, peach, nectarine or mango slices.

Serves 6 – 8

-CARAMELIZED RICE PUDDING-

$^1/_4$ cup short-grain rice
3 tablespoons superfine sugar
1 teaspoon natural vanilla extract
grated rind of 1 lemon
1 cinnamon stick (optional)
3 cups milk
4 tablespoons brown sugar

Place the rice in the soaked clay pot. Add the superfine sugar, vanilla, lemon rind, cinnamon stick (if used) and milk. Cover the pot and place in the cold oven. Set the oven at 375F. Cook for 2 – 2$^1/_2$ hours, or until the pudding is thick and creamy, stirring occasionally.

Increase the oven setting to 475F. Discard the cinnamon stick. Smooth the surface of the pudding, then sprinkle the brown sugar over it in an even layer. Cook, uncovered, for 5 – 8 minutes, or until the brown sugar is melted and lightly caramelized. Serve at once.

Serves 6

—FRENCH-STYLE MILK ROLLS—

2 cups all-purpose flour
$^1/_2$ teaspoon salt
1 tablespoon lard
$^1/_2$ cup milk
1 teaspoon superfine sugar
2 teaspoons dried yeast

Place the flour in a bowl with the salt, then rub in the lard. Heat the milk until just lukewarm, then stir in the sugar and sprinkle the yeast over the top. Set aside in a warm place, without stirring, for about 15 minutes until the yeast liquid is frothy.

Cut two pieces of non-stick baking parchment to fit in the bottom of the clay pot. Pour the yeast liquid into the flour mixture and mix to a soft dough. Knead briefly until smooth, then replace in the bowl, cover and leave in a warm place until doubled in size. Turn out and knead very briefly, then divide into quarters. Shape each piece into a long roll which fits into the clay pot. Place two rolls on each piece of parchment on a board and leave in a warm place to rise. Meanwhile, soak the clay pot.

Transfer two of the rolls to the pot on their paper. Cover the pot and place in the cold oven. Set the oven at 475F. Cook for 40 minutes. Uncover the pot and cook for a further 5 minutes. Bake the remaining rolls in the same way. Cool on a wire rack.

Makes 4

BRAIDED BREAD

oil for greasing
4 cups bread flour
1 teaspoon salt
2 tablespoons margarine or lard
1 sachet easy-blend yeast
1/2 cup hand-hot milk
beaten egg, to glaze
1 tablespoon poppy seeds

Place the flour and salt in a bowl. Rub in the margarine or lard, then mix in the yeast. Mix in 1 cup hand-hot water to make a firm dough. Knead the dough for about 10 minutes, until it is smooth and elastic. Divide the dough into three, then roll each piece into a long, thin rope. Attach the ropes of dough at one end, then braid them together into a wide, plump braid.

Place the braid in the lined clay pot, plumping it up neatly, then leave in a warm place until doubled in size. Brush with beaten egg and sprinkle with poppy seeds. Cover the pot and place in the cold oven. Set the oven at 450F. Cook for 50 minutes. Uncover the pot and cook for a further 10 minutes. Transfer to a wire rack to cool.

Makes 1 large loaf

SAVORY SAUSAGE LOAF

oil for greasing
4 cups bread flour
1 teaspoon salt
2 tablespoons margarine or lard
1 sachet easy-blend yeast
1 tablespoon dried marjoram
3 kielbasa or about 3/4 pound smoked sausage or
    spicy cooked sausage

Line the bottom of the soaked clay pot with non-stick baking parchment. Grease the sides well with oil. Place the flour and salt in a bowl. Rub in the shortening, then mix in the yeast and marjoram. Mix in 1 cup hand-hot water to make a firm dough.

Knead the dough for about 10 minutes, until it is smooth and elastic. Flatten the dough, place the kielbasa or sausage in the middle, then wrap the dough around it and pinch the ends together, kneading them to seal the dough around the sausage. Place the dough into the pot, sealed edges down. Leave in a warm place until doubled in size.

Cover the pot and place in the cold oven. Set the oven at 450°F. Cook for 50 minutes. Uncover the pot and cook for a further 10 minutes. Transfer to a wire rack to cool, then serve warm, cut into thick slices.

Makes 1 large loaf

CORNBREAD

1 1/2 cups cornmeal
1/2 cup all-purpose flour
1 teaspoon salt
1 teaspoon baking powder
1 teaspoon bicarbonate of soda
1/4 cup melted butter
2 cups milk
juice of 1/2 lemon
2 eggs
oil for greasing

Mix together the cornmeal, flour, salt, baking powder and bicarbonate of soda. Make a well in the middle. Pour in the melted butter, milk, lemon juice and eggs, then beat well to make a smooth, thick batter. Thoroughly grease the soaked clay pot and pour in the batter. Cover the pot and place in the cold oven.

Set the oven at 450F. Cook for 30 minutes. Uncover the pot and cook for a further 5 minutes, or until the bread is firm to the touch and golden-brown. Insert a metal skewer into the middle of the bread – if it comes out sticky with mixture, the bread is not cooked. Serve warm as an accompaniment for stews and similar savory dishes.

Serves 8

ZUCCHINI LOAF

oil for greasing
2 cups self-rising flour
$^1/_2$ cup margarine or butter
1 teaspoon cinnamon
$^1/_2$ cup superfine sugar
$^3/_4$ cup golden raisins
1 cup chopped walnuts
1 cup peeled and finely grated zucchini (see note)
1 egg
$^1/_2$ cup milk

Line the bottom of the soaked clay pot with non-stick baking parchment. Grease the sides of the pot. Place the flour in a bowl. Rub in the shortening, then stir in the cinnamon, sugar, golden raisins and walnuts. Add the zucchini and mix well so that they are evenly distributed. Beat in the egg and milk to make a soft mixture. Turn into the pot and smooth the top.

Cover the pot and place in the cold oven. Set the oven at 400F. Cook for 1 hour. Uncover the pot and cook for a further 8 – 10 minutes for extra crispness. Insert a metal skewer into the bread – if it has any sticky mixture on it, the loaf is not cooked. Cool on a wire rack, serve sliced and buttered.

Makes 1 large loaf

Note: Squeeze excess moisture from the grated zucchini before measuring them.

─CHOCOLATE HONEY SWIRL─

3 cups bread flour
$1/2$ teaspoon salt
$1/3$ cup butter
3 tablespoons superfine sugar
$3/4$ cup milk
3 teaspoons dried yeast
$1/2$ pound chocolate chips
3 tablespoons clear honey
2 tablespoons raisins
2 tablespoons chopped candied citron peel
4 tablespoons chopped nuts (pecans, walnuts, hazelnuts or others)
2 teaspoons ground cinnamon
confectioners' sugar, to sift

Place the flour and salt in a bowl, then rub in the butter. Stir in most of the sugar. Heat the milk until just lukewarm, then stir in the remaining sugar and sprinkle the yeast over the top. Set aside in a warm place, without stirring, for about 15 minutes until frothy. Pour the yeast liquid into the flour mixture and mix to a soft dough. Knead for 10 minutes, then replace in the bowl, cover and leave in a warm place until doubled in size. Meanwhile, mix the remaining ingredients.

Knead the dough briefly, then roll it out into an oval, about $1/2$ inch thick. Spread the chocolate mixture over, leaving a border. Dampen the edge, then roll up the dough. Pinch the edge to seal it well. Place non-stick baking parchment in the soaked pot and put the loaf in it. Cover and leave in a warm place until doubled. Place in the cold oven. Set the oven at 450F. Cook for 45 minutes. Uncover and cook for 10 minutes. Cool on a rack. Sift with confectioners' sugar.

Makes 1 loaf

TARRAGON SCALLOPS

¹/₂ cup butter
16 scallops, shelled
2 tablespoons chopped tarragon
1 scallion, chopped
1 tablespoon chopped parsley
3 slices bread, crusts removed and quartered
    diagonally
¹/₂ cup sour cream
salt and pepper
tarragon sprigs, to garnish

Microwave Method
Place half the butter in a small bowl and melt on full power for 1 minute. Place the scallops in the soaked clay pot, add the tarragon, scallion, parsley and butter. Cover the pot and cook on medium power for about 10 minutes, stirring once, until the scallops are just cooked – they should be firm but not toughened.

Meanwhile heat the remaining butter in a skillet and fry the bread until golden on both sides. Transfer to warmed serving plates. Stir the sour cream into the scallops with seasoning to taste and cook for 1 minute on medium power. Spoon over the triangular croûtons and serve garnished with tarragon sprigs.

Serves 4

Note: Shelled, uncooked large shrimp may be used instead of scallops.

PAELLA

1 onion, chopped
2 garlic cloves, crushed
1 green sweet pepper, seeded and chopped
2 chorizo, thinly sliced
2 boneless chicken breasts, skinned and diced
3/4 pound long-grain rice
1/2 teaspoon powdered saffron
2 1/2 cups chicken stock
1/2 cup dry white wine
salt and pepper
3/4 pound peeled, cooked shrimp
1/2 pound shelled, cooked mussels (frozen are fine)
plenty of chopped parsley

Microwave Method

Mix the onion, garlic, pepper, chorizo and chicken in the soaked clay pot. Cover the pot and cook on full power for 15 minutes. Stir in the rice and saffron, then pour in the stock and wine. Add seasoning. Cook, covered, on full power for 15 minutes, stir, then reduce the setting to medium power and cook for a further 15 minutes.

Frozen shrimp and mussels should be thawed. Sprinkle them over the rice and cook, covered, for a further 10 minutes on medium power. Fork the shrimp, mussels and parsley into the rice, taste for seasoning and serve. Crusty bread and salad are the only accompaniments necessary.

Serves 4

MICROWAVE CHICKEN RISOTTO

1 onion, chopped
1 red sweet pepper, seeded and chopped
2 tablespoons oil
3 boneless chicken breasts, skinned and cubed
1 garlic clove, crushed
1 bay leaf
$^1/_4$ pound mushrooms, sliced
$^3/_4$ pound long-grain rice
1 cup dry white wine
2 cups chicken stock
salt and pepper
4 – 6 tablespoons freshly grated Parmesan cheese
2 tablespoons chopped parsley
$^1/_2$ cup light cream (optional)
parsley sprig, to garnish

Microwave Method
Mix the onion, sweet pepper, oil, chicken and garlic in the soaked clay pot. Add the bay leaf. Cover the pot and cook on full power for 10 minutes. Add the mushrooms and rice, stir to combine all the ingredients and coat the rice in the juices. Pour in the wine and stock, then add seasoning. Cook, covered, on full power for 15 minutes.

Stir lightly, reduce the setting to medium power and cook for 35 minutes. Leave to stand, still covered, for 5 minutes. The rice should be tender and the risotto moist. Check that the chicken is cooked and taste for seasoning. Stir in the cheese, parsley and cream (if used), and cook, covered, on full power for 2 minutes. Leave to stand for 2 minutes before forking up the grains and serving, garnished with parsley.

Serves 4

—SPAGHETTI WITH CHICKEN—

2 tablespoons olive oil
1 large onion, chopped
1 green sweet pepper, seeded and chopped
1 garlic clove, crushed
4 tablespoons tomato paste
$^1/_2$ cup red wine
$^1/_2$ cup chicken stock
4 tomatoes, peeled and roughly chopped
$^1/_4$ pound mushrooms, sliced
1 bay leaf
salt and pepper
4 boneless chicken breasts, skinned and sliced
$^3/_4$ pound spaghetti
handful of basil leaves, shredded
freshly grated Parmesan cheese, to serve

Microwave Method

Mix together the oil, onion, sweet pepper and garlic in a bowl. Cover the bowl and cook on full power for 5 minutes. Stir in the tomato paste, wine and stock. Place the tomatoes, mushrooms and bay leaf in the soaked clay pot. Season well, then arrange the chicken slices on top. Pour the onion mixture over. Cover the pot and cook on full power for 10 minutes. Stir well, then reduce the setting to medium power and cook for a further 20 minutes, stirring once.

Meanwhile, lower the spaghetti into a pan of boiling salted water and bring back to a boil. Boil for 15 minutes, or until just tender. Drain and divide between serving plates. Ladle the chicken mixture over the top and sprinkle with basil. Serve with Parmesan cheese.

Serves 4

BRAISED STEAK

1 onion, chopped
1 carrot, halved and sliced
2 tablespoons oil
1 1/2 pounds rump steak
1 tablespoon all-purpose flour
1 cup beef stock
1/2 pound mushrooms, sliced
dash of Worcestershire sauce
1 bay leaf
salt and pepper
parsley sprigs, to garnish

Microwave Method
Place the onion and carrot in a bowl. Mix in the oil, cover the bowl and cook on full power for 5 minutes. Meanwhile, cut the meat across the grain into small thin slices – about 1 – 2-inches square. Place the steak in the soaked clay pot. Stir the flour into the onion mixture, then gradually mix in the stock. Pour this over the meat. Add the mushrooms, Worcestershire sauce and bay leaf. Cover the pot and cook on full power for 15 minutes.

Reduce the setting to medium power and cook for a further 45 minutes, stirring twice, until the steak is tender. Leave to stand, without removing the lid, for 10 minutes. Taste for seasoning, sprinkle with parsley and serve.

Serves 4

MARINATED LAMB

2 pounds lean, boneless leg of lamb
2 garlic cloves, crushed
juice of 1 lemon
1 teaspoon oregano
$1/2$ cup red wine
2 tablespoons olive oil
1 onion, chopped
1 tablespoon tomato paste
2 teaspoons sugar
4 cups peeled and roughly chopped tomatoes
$1/2$ cup chicken stock
salt and pepper
$1/4$ pound mushrooms, sliced
1 bay leaf

Microwave Method
Cut the lamb into small thin slices as for the beef (see opposite). Place in a bowl. Add the garlic, lemon juice, oregano and wine. Mix well, cover and leave for 1 – 2 days in the refrigerator, stirring occasionally. Place the oil and onion in a bowl and cook on full power for 3 minutes. Add the tomato paste, sugar, tomatoes, stock and seasoning.

Place the meat and its marinade in the soaked clay pot. Top with the mushrooms, then pour in the onion mixture. Add the bay leaf. Cover the pot and cook on full power for 15 minutes. Stir, then reduce the setting to medium power and cook, covered, for a further 45 minutes, or until the meat is tender, stirring twice. Leave to stand for 10 minutes before serving. Buttered noodles and green beans are excellent accompaniments.

Serves 4

— SWEET-SOUR PORK CHOPS —

1 onion, halved and sliced
1 carrot, halved and cut into thin strips
1 green sweet pepper, seeded, halved and sliced
2 tablespoons oil
2 tablespoons tomato ketchup
2 tablespoons soy sauce
2 tablespoons dry sherry
1 teaspoon sesame oil
4 pork chops, trimmed of fat
1 teaspoon cornstarch
1 tablespoon wine vinegar
1 tablespoon sugar
1 can (8-ounce) pineapple chunks
parsley sprigs, to garnish

Microwave Method
Mix the onion, carrot, pepper and oil in a bowl. Cover the bowl and cook on full power for 5 minutes. Stir in the ketchup, soy sauce, sherry and sesame oil. Lay the chops in the soaked clay pot. Spoon the vegetable mixture over them. Cover the pot and cook on full power for 15 minutes. Turn the chops, reduce the setting to medium power and cook, covered, for a further 25 minutes, or until the chops are cooked through.

Meanwhile, mix the cornstarch with the wine vinegar and sugar. Add 2 tablespoons of the syrup from the pineapple, pour this mixture into the pot and mix it with the cooking juices. Add the drained pineapple. Cook, covered, for a final 5 minutes to thicken the sauce. Leave to stand for 5 minutes before serving, garnished with parsley sprigs.

Serves 4

MICROWAVE MEATLOAF

1 pound ground pork
1 pound ground beef
2 cups fresh bread crumbs
salt and pepper
1 onion, grated
2 tablespoons chopped parsley
1 teaspoon mixed dried herbs
1 egg, beaten
1 tablespoon tomato paste
1 tablespoon mustard
salad ingredients, to garnish

Microwave Method
Mix the pork and beef with the bread crumbs. Add plenty of seasoning, the onion, parsley, herbs, egg, tomato paste and mustard. Pound the ingredients together until they are thoroughly combined.

Turn the mixture into the soaked clay pot. Cover the pot and cook on full power for 10 minutes. Reduce the setting to medium power and cook for a further 30 minutes. Leave to stand for 10 minutes without un-covering the dish. Then pierce the middle of the meatloaf with the point of a knife to check that it is cooked. Serve sliced, with salad and new or baked potatoes. Garnish with salad ingredients.

Serves 8

INDEX